FaithSongs

Leader's Edition

Abingdon Press
Nashville

FAITHSONGS
Leader's Edition

Copyright © 2003 Abingdon Press

This book is printed on acid-free, recycled paper.

ISBN 13: 978-0-687-04579-2

Scripture quotations, unless otherwise marked, are from the New Revised Standard Version Bible, copyright © 1989 by the Division of Christian Education of the National Council of the Churches of Christ in the USA.

11 12 — 10 9 8 7 6 5 4

Contents

Introduction

FaithSongs was created to enhance the participation of children in worship through the gift of music. In the midst of their busy lives, children need to hear and learn songs that remind us all to "Be Still and Know," to "Come Into God's Presence Singing," to "Light One Candle for Waiting," and to say "How Majestic Is Your Name." Singing enables each of us to praise God in a way that involves our whole being. These songs become the stories of our faith—our faith songs.

The Editions

In this *FaithSongs Leader's Edition* you will find teaching ideas, background information and suggestions on using these songs in worship and educational settings. Additionally, many of the leader's helps include suggested movements or dramatic possibilities. Use these leader's helps as a starting place for the many ways you can teach and use these songs.

Chords symbols are included so you can add a variety of instruments or use the chords to improvise on the printed accompaniment. In many cases you will need to simplify the chords for use with guitar, handchimes, handbells, or instrumental ensembles, such as praise bands. You know the skills of those who will be serving together with you, and we encourage you to make adaptations as needed to fit your setting.

Indexes include topical, scriptural, CD tracks, and title/first line. These tools will help you choose the songs that will best fit the abilities of your children and the needs of your worship setting. Additionally, you will find information on where to contact the copyright holders in the Acknowledgments.

Look for the book icon near the title of each song in the Leader's Edition. The number in the icon will quickly alert you to the page number of the same song in the Singer's Edition.

The *FaithSongs Singer's Edition* includes the vocal line and the text for each song. This edition is a useful tool that will help your singers learn the songs, read the texts as prayers, and enhance their music education.

The *FaithSongs CD set* is in split-track format. This gives you many options in using the CDs for rehearsal and in worship. Every song in *FaithSongs* has been recorded for you.

A Children's Choir Curriculum

Using *FaithSongs* and your hymnal as the core materials for your children's choir ministry, you can easily create your own children's choir curriculum. This allows you to have complete control over what songs are chosen and how they will be introduced and learned. Whether you are a first-time children's music leader or have many years of experience, you can tailor your curriculum to meet the specific needs of your choir each year. You can choose from the variety of leader's helps to create your own curriculum:

1. Choose the music for your choir for the choir year. Include songs from *FaithSongs* as well as hymns/songs from your hymnal. You can even add a separate octavo for a special Sunday if desired. Remember, with *FaithSongs* you choose your own repertoire to fit both your children's choir and worship needs.

2. Decide how you will teach and lead each song using the helps and ideas for the songs you have chosen.

3. Fill out a rehearsal planning worksheet

for your rehearsals. (See page 196 for a reproducible worksheet or create your own.)

4. Develop a choir year theme for the songs you have chosen for a specific year and use this throughout the year for recruitment and communication.

A Songbook for Educational Settings

The leader's helps in *FaithSongs* will enable you to use many of the songs in Sunday schools, assembly times, vacation Bible schools, after-school programs, and other settings. Use the scriptural or topical index to choose the song for the session, then enjoy singing together. You can also select one or more of the helps to enhance learning through movement, additional text study ideas, and more. Many of the helps can be quickly turned into a fun musical game with the children. Use the recordings as a learning tool if you are uncomfortable leading the children in singing. The exciting instrumentation will have your children singing along in no time! Begin building a repertoire of songs that your children can sing together. Many of the suggested uses will fit within your educational setting as well as in worship. Consider learning the songs in your educational setting, then using the song in worship with the congregation.

The *FaithSongs* Recording

The *FaithSongs* split-track CD set can be used in a variety of ways:

- Use the CD to learn the song and to consider possible arrangement or stanza choices.
- Use the voices-only channel as a teaching tool to help your children clearly hear the melody. Use the CD as a leader's help when playing the games or tapping, clapping, or moving to the music.
- Play some of the children's favorite songs as they enter your room to help create a welcoming environment.
- Use the accompaniment-only channel in rehearsal to listen for secure texts and melodies.
- Use the accompaniment-only channel as accompaniment in rehearsal and/or worship settings.
- Use the CD with a portable CD player as accompaniment when visiting nursing homes or other situations when there is no piano or accompanist available.
- Use the musical arrangements on the CD as a model with your own instrumental ensemble or praise band. Instrumentation on the CD includes keyboards, guitars, percussion, bass, and woodwinds.
- Which verses? By turning the voice track down you can sing the stanzas that are most appropriate to your setting for a specific experience. When singing only one stanza in rehearsal, ask a helper to push the pause button or turn down the volume at the end of the stanza. Remember, you can turn the voice track down and practice the words to the same stanza several times by singing to the instrumental track only.
- Canons and rounds: How many canon voices can your group sing comfortably? In most cases the CD instrumental version is recorded so you can sing the total number of possible parts noted with a melody instrument to help the extra voice parts.
- Part singing: The second voice part is played on the instrumental accompaniment. One way to use this to help teach the second part is to turn down the voices and ask your singers to listen for the solo instrument playing that part.

Movement Ideas

Movement adds a visual interpretation to the children's singing. For many children, their preferred learning style is through movement. There will be children in your ministry who love music and need to move as a part of their musical expression. Many songs in *FaithSongs* have simple movements included. Several suggest that you consider adding movements of your own creation or include sign language options.

Anyone can do the simple movements included in *FaithSongs*, even a person with two left feet! If you feel uncomfortable teaching the movements, ask one of the children to learn the movements in advance and to lead the group in the movement; what a wonderful way for children to share their talent! If you discover you have a child who is a "natural" in moving, ask that child to create movements for you. Give them simple guidelines: space limitations, architectural concerns, such as steps or furniture in the area, and a gentle reminder that the group has to be able to sing and move at the same time.

Sign Language

The sign language suggestions given in *FaithSongs* are designed to be used as a teaching tool to help the children remember specific portions of a text or to enhance the visual interpretation of the song. We suggest that you contact someone in your community who is experienced in sign language and ask them to come and teach the sign language, especially if you decide to sign the entire text. You can contact your local school system or a local community organization for persons with hearing impairment for names of persons who may be able to help you. There are several sign language books available, such as *The Joy of Signing* by Lottie L. Riekehof (Springfield, Mo.: Gospel Publishing House, 1987) or *Religious Signing, A Comprehensive Guide for All Faiths* by Elaine Costello (New York: Bantam Books, 1986). Contact your local library or bookstore.

Reproducible Teaching Pages

We have included two reproducible teaching pages to help you as you share your joy of music with your choir. Use these as "idea generators" and you will be creating your own teaching aids in no time.

Doxology Word Scramble (page 79)

- Make copies for your group and ask them to unscramble the text. This learning activity can be created easily for most songs.

Code Word Game: "Things We Do In Choir" (page 191)

- Make copies for your group and ask them to use the code to fill in the blanks. This is a fun way to learn the texts of songs. Create your own code word games by using music symbols, shapes, Christian symbols, or other small pictures as keys to the code.

Delight and Joy

There is so much joy to be found as a leader of children's music. Expect the unexpected! Delight in the gifts of each child! You will discover a new understanding of what it means to be disciples of Christ as you sing your faith together!

Debi Tyree
Project Editor

Meet the Writers*

David Bone, Editorial Consultant, Helps Text Editor, is the administrator of The Fellowship of United Methodists in Music and Worship Arts. David is also co-author of the annual publications *The United Methodist Music and Worship Planner* and *Prepare! A Weekly Worship Planbook.* He serves as a clinician on the national level and was an editor of *Church Music for Children.* David is a member of West End UMC in Nashville, Tennessee, where he directs the older elementary children's choir and sings in the Chancel Choir.

Kathy Evans, Helps Writer, currently serves as Director of Children's and Youth Music Ministry at Markum Woods Presbyterian Church in Lake Mary, Florida. She also serves as an instructor in the Community School of Music at Rollins College and as Coordinator and Director of the Bach Festival Children's Choir—both in Winter Park, Florida. She has served churches in Tennessee, Georgia, and Florida and is a nationally recognized clinician in church music.

John D. Horman, Helps Writer, completed twenty-five years of service to the Montgomery County, Maryland public school system prior to his retirement in 1995. He also celebrated his twenty-fifth anniversary as Director of Music at Warner Memorial Presbyterian Church in Silver Spring, Maryland. He is in constant demand as a workshop clinician throughout the country, and his compositions are found in the catalogs of numerous national music publishers. He served six years on the Choristers Guild board of directors, the last two as president, served three years as an editor of Abingdon's *Church Music for Children* music curriculum, and is the composer of the Christmas musicals *What Child Was This?* and *The Angel Band* also published by Abingdon Press.

Nylea L. Butler-Moore, Helps Writer, is the Music Director for the alternative worship service at Valencia United Methodist Church in Valencia, California. A conductor, vocalist, and keyboardist, she also composes, arranges, and edits music for several publishers. Among her most recent publications are the session plan components of the musicals, *Showdown at Dry Gulch, The Angel Band,* and *Follow That Star!* as well as the MIDI version of *The Faith We Sing*—all published by Abingdon Press.

Debi Tyree, Project Editor and Helps Writer, is a Music Resources Development Editor for Abingdon Press. Debi is an ordained deacon in The United Methodist Church and lives in Nashville, Tennessee. She has also served as Associate Minister of Music and Worship Arts Ministries at Shady Grove United Methodist Church, where she directed a program of twelve choirs from kindergarten to seniors for over twenty years. Currently, she is active in her local church, where she serves as a children's choir director. She has written a variety of articles and other publications, including the session plans to the Abingdon Press musicals *No Doubt About It!* and *What Child Was This?* She compiled and edited the collection *With Heart and Hands and Voices*, also published by Abingdon Press.

 **Ginger G. Wyrick,** Helps Writer, is Director of Choral Activities at Queens University, Charlotte, North Carolina. She also serves as music and liturgical arts consultant to churches and church-related events offer-

ing staff and program development. She is frequently sought after as guest conductor and clinician at various workshops. Ginger has also written the younger elementary age levels of all three years of Abingdon's *Church Music for Children* curriculum, as well as *The Choir Member's Companion* and *Church Choir 101*, a resource for teaching the fundamentals of church music to choir members.

* The initials at the end of each song's helps designate which writer wrote helps for that song.

Signing for "Lord, Make Me More Holy," page 91

Holy

Loving

Patient

Faithful

Amen

5 Come into God's Presence Singing

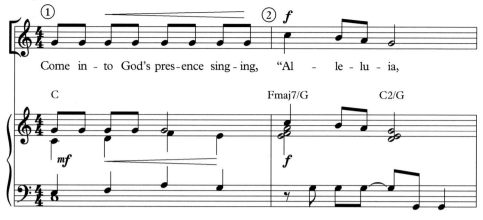

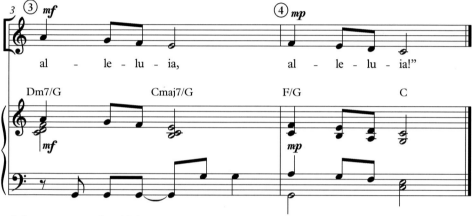

Other stanzas may be added:
    "Jesus is Lord." *(Easter, Ascension)*
    "Worthy the Lamb." *(Lent)*
    "Glory to God." *(Christmas)*

Final stanza each time (especially appropriate to sing as a round):
    Praise the Lord together singing, "Alleluia, …"

WORDS: Anonymous
MUSIC: Anonymous, arr. by John D. Horman
Arr. © 2003 Abingdon Press, admin. by The Copyright Co., Nashville, TN 37212

Alleluia

Entering into worship may take on different forms and attitudes. In this song, we join with the psalmist as we come before God singing "Alleluia," "Jesus is Lord," "Worthy the Lamb," and "Glory to God." Read Psalm 95 and list what we can do as we enter into worship.

This general call to worship is easy to teach because of its short, repetitive structure. Note the musical sequence in measures 2-4. Illustrate the descending stepwise pattern and how the composer lowers the starting note for each use.

Other Ideas:
- Add sign language for the word "Alleluia" each time it is sung.
- Sing as a round. Start with two groups and work up to four groups. (Since the round results in thirds, some groups may have difficulty.)
- Sing as a general gathering song or call to worship. Extract stanzas as seasonal responses: "Jesus is Lord" on Easter or Ascension; "Worthy the Lamb" during Lent or Holy Week; and "Glory to God" during Christmas.
- Create a "Scale Ladder." Consider drawing a ladder with eight steps on a piece of posterboard. Move your hand up and down the ladder steps to illustrate the pattern as you sing. You could also tape a series of eight copies of an interesting drawing on the wall in a vertical line (leaves, apples, Christmas trees, soccer balls) to create a "Scale Picture." Tap the pictures with your hand to show the pattern of the melody line.

(GW)

Gather the people together for worship using this song in the Shona language of Zimbabwe. Patrick Matsikenyiri, composer and Professor of Music at Africa University, teaches this song by singing each phrase in a call and response pattern between leader and the group. He quickly moves to singing the entire song together using the leader phrase at the end of the song to indicate the next text that will be sung.

Shona Pronunciation Guide:
JEH-soo, TAH-wah PAH-noh; moo-ZEE-tah REH-nyoo; MAHM-boh JEH-soo.

This song is usually sung unaccompanied or with a simple percussion pattern played by a *hosho*. A hosho is an African instrument made from a maranka gourd with hota seeds inside. It looks much like maracas but has a very knobby skin rather than smooth skin.

Play a constant eighth note to keep the underlying pulse of the song, using maracas if you don't have a hosho. A light drum can also be used.

Other Ideas:
• You may add new stanzas by substituting the words "Jesu" and "Jesus" with "Savior" or "Spirit" or other names for Jesus or the Holy Spirit. The leader makes this transition in the text as they sing "Welcome, Savior" instead of "Welcome, Jesu." The children will follow the leader; no announcements or books are needed.

(DT)

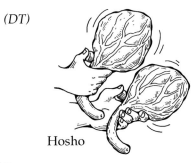

Hosho

Jesu, Tawa Pano
(Jesus, We Are Here)

6

Optional verses:
2. Savior, … 3. Master, … 4. Spirit, …

*Melody note sometimes sung as B while middle C is sometimes played as D♯.
**Omit last time.
WORDS: Patrick Matsikenyiri
MUSIC: Patrick Matsikenyiri; descant by Jorge Lockwood
© 1990, 1996 General Board of Global Ministries, GBGMusik

Praising God • Gathering

Come, Let Us Gather

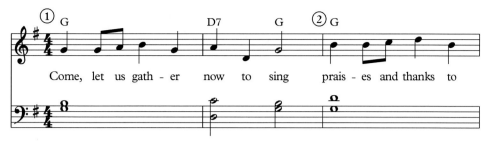

Come, let us gath-er now to sing prais-es and thanks to

God, our King. God's _ love is great-er than an-y-thing.

Orff Instrument Patterns

Triangle or Soprano Glockenspiel

Alto Xylophone

Alto Glockenspiel

Bass Xylophone

WORDS: Traditional
MUSIC: Traditional, arr. by Richard L. Van Oss
Arr. © 1994 CRC Publications

Discuss possible reasons we gather to worship. Could the last line of the song—"God's love is greater than any-thing"—provide a primary rea-son?

Play the "Line or Space" game. Divide the children into two or more teams. Ask the first team to determine whether the first note in the melody is on a line or a space (Line); then ask the second team to make the same determination for the second note in the melody. Repeat the process until all the notes in the melody have been examined. Award one point for each correct answer.

If time allows, move to the "Step or Skip" phase of the game. Explain that the notes of a melody can move up or down the staff in two ways: by steps or by skips. Stepwise notes move from one line to the next space or from one space to the next line. Skips are jumps of more than a step. Ask the teams to determine if the move-ment between one note and the adjacent one is a step, skip, or repeated note.

Teach the concept of a "scale," using the fifth measure of the song as an example of a descending scale.

Other Ideas:
• Sing in three-part canon, or use instruments to play one or more parts as the children sing.
• Use as a gathering song, a general call to worship, or as part of a Thanksgiving cele-bration.
• Use a "Scale Ladder" to visu-ally show the rise and fall of the pitches of the melody. See "Other Ideas" on page 9 for directions.

(NB)

The syncopated accompaniment immediately gives rhythmic energy to this joyful song. The repetition of the opening text makes this easy to teach in either language. Children will enjoy the international flavor, especially with the addition of instruments.

Spanish Pronunciation Guide:
VEH-need kahn-TEH-moss
ahl SEH-nyor
COHN ah-leh-GREE-ah

Add instruments during the introduction and refrain sections only:

Claves:

Finger cymbals or triangle:

Drum:

Maracas:

L. R. L. R.   L. R. L. R.

Other Ideas:
• Sing this as a call to worship or gathering song. The refrain may be used as an antiphon with the reading of Psalm 95.
• Create rhythm cards to teach syncopation. Put the numbers and circles on side 1 of the card and the corresponding rhythmic notation on side 2. Count aloud all the numbers, but clap only the first of each circled number set. Once the children can clap the pattern accurately, display the rhythmic notation (opposite side of the card) and clap. Locate examples of card 4 and card 5 in the music and sing.

(GW)

Venid Cantemos
(Come, Let Us Sing)

8

Pronounced: Veh-need kahn-teh-moss ahl Seh-nyor cone ah-le-gree-ah

WORDS: Based on Psalm 95:1-7
MUSIC: Raquel M. Martínez

Praising God • Giving Thanks and Praise

Anthem Setting: "Venid Cantemos" by Raquel M. Martínez (Abingdon Press, 061679). Unison voices and keyboard with optional percussion.

S. C. Molefe wrote this song to be used as the "Amen" at the end of the Great Thanksgiving or Communion prayer. This was one of Molefe's first formal compositions. Former South African President Nelson Mandela is a member of the Xhosa tribe.

Xhosa Pronunciation Guide:

ah-MEN see-YAH-koo-DOO-mee-SAH

ah-MEN bah-WOH (mah-SEE-tee)

(*Bawo* means "Amen.")

Say each phrase of the song, asking the children to repeat the text. Begin swaying and singing the song, encouraging the children to sing with you. Once they are comfortable with the melody and text, begin singing the Leader part to give them cues to continue singing.

Move back and forth between the English and Xhosa text, building in joy and intensity each time until everyone joins together on the final "Amen Siyakudumisa!"

Other Ideas:

• Sing this with lots of energy and joy, using a strong steady beat. Traditional Xhosa music doesn't use drums, but movement is important. Add a simple sway: small step right, close with left foot; small step left, close with right foot. Repeat this movement as you sing. (This movement will take two measures.)

• Use this song as a choir processional by having the children sway together in tempo and then singing and moving into the aisles of the worship space. Once the children have moved to the front of the worship space, invite the congregation to join in the singing.

(DT)

Amen Siakudumisa
(Amen, We Praise Your Name, O God)

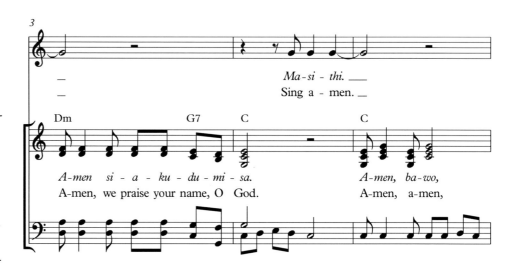

WORDS: Trad. Xhosa (South Africa) attr. to S. C. Molefe as taught by George Mxadana
MUSIC: Trad. Xhosa melody (South Africa) attr. to S. C. Molefe as taught by George Mxadana
© 1996 General Board of Global Ministries, GBGMusik

Praising God • Giving Thanks and Praise

Father, I Adore You

10

May be sung as a canon.

2. Jesus, I adore you …
3. Spirit, I adore you …

WORDS: Terrye Coehlo Strom
MUSIC: Terrye Coehlo Strom
© 1972 CCCM Music, admin. by Maranatha! Music c/o The Copyright Company, Nashville, TN 37212. All rights
reserved. International copyright secured. Used by permission.

Ask the children what it means to "adore" someone or something. Why should we adore God? What does it mean to lay our lives before God? What are some of the reasons we love God?

The construction of the text celebrates the Trinity: stanza 1 is sung to the Father; stanza 2 is sung to the Son ("Jesus"); and stanza 3 is sung to the Holy Spirit.

Provide a simple explanation of the Trinity by drawing three interlocking circles (an ancient Christian symbol for the Trinity) on a chart. The Trinity is like these circles in that you can see all three individually, but together they make one whole. Each one is important to the overall design. Each part of the Godhead is unique but necessary to the whole personage of God.

Other Ideas:
• This song works well with guitar or worship band.
• Sing in unison or in a three-part canon.
• For visual impact, add sign language for Father, Jesus, and Spirit.
• Consider adding simple flowing hand and arm movements for the text.
• The example on the *FaithSongs* CD is sung in unison; however, the instrumental track will allow you to sing this as a three-part round.

(NB)

Father

Jesus

Spirit

The guardianship of God is the theme of this song. There are many phrases in the text that are worth repeating: "the Lord is near me," "never will I fear," "for the Lord is near," "everywhere I go."

Develop a choral speaking introduction using these phrases. Divide the children into groups and choose three to four phrases to overlap and speak together. Create a mini-composition and follow it with the introduction. Repeat as an interlude and/or coda. Remind the children to use the higher pitch range of their speaking voice.

The song uses notes of three different lengths. Speak the words in rhythm and assign these note lengths to specific body percussions:

Eighth notes = Alternating snaps or alternating patschen (patting the thighs)
Quarter notes = Claps
Whole note = Slide palms slowly down to knees

Other Ideas:

• The idea of "fear" in today's world and the security of God's presence are themes that will generate much discussion with children. Make the distinction between "God keeps you *from* all harm" and "God is with us to help us and strengthen us *in* our hardships."

• Tell the children about the composer. Natalie Sleeth was a very successful composer. Many children will be familiar with her song, "Hymn of Promise." Some of your singers' parents probably sang her music when they were in children's choirs. She died on the first day of spring in 1992.

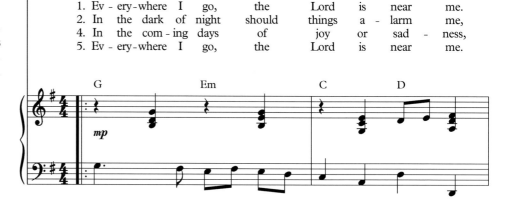

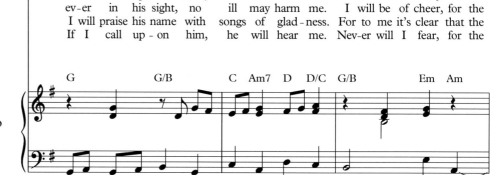

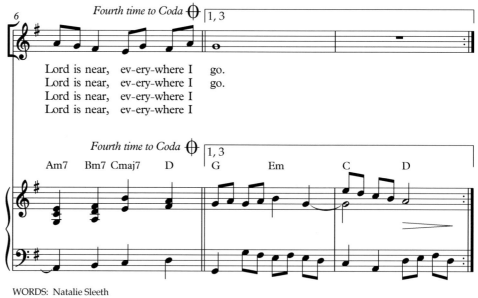

WORDS: Natalie Sleeth
MUSIC: Natalie Sleeth
© 1975 Choristers Guild

Praising God • Giving Thanks and Praise

(JH)

Anthem Setting: "Everywhere I Go" by Natalie Sleeth (Choristers Guild, CGA-171). Unison voices with keyboard and optional second part.

Prayers take on many forms. Whether petition, praise, sorrow, or blessing, the prayer life of the Christian communicates the desires of the heart.

The simple descending melody is easy to teach. Model the melodic direction with your hand as you sing, or assign scale numbers/solfège to each pitch. Identify and demonstrate the octave leap and the upbeat/partial measure.

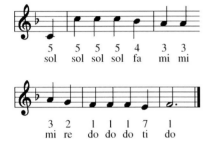

Other Ideas:
- Invite the children to create additional stanzas. They may choose to insert names of people as stanzas.
- Sing as a round.
- Sing this as a general prayer in worship, choir, Sunday school, or other gathering. Use stanza 3 as a response to prayer in worship.
- Encourage children to sing this at home before a meal or at bedtime.
- Use a "Scale Ladder" to visually show the rise and fall of the pitches of the melody. See "Other Ideas" on page 9 for directions.
- The example on the *FaithSongs* CD is sung in unison on stanzas 1-3; however, the instrumental track will allow you to sing this as a three-part canon.

(GW)

For Health and Strength

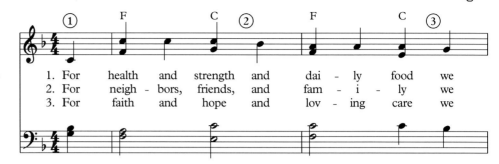

1. For health and strength and dai - ly food we
2. For neigh - bors, friends, and fam - i - ly we
3. For faith and hope and lov - ing care we

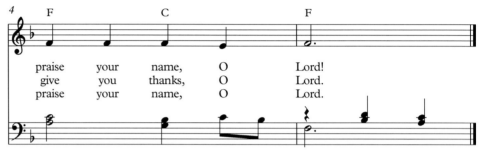

praise your name, O Lord!
give you thanks, O Lord.
praise your name, O Lord.

Omit accompaniment when sung as a round.

WORDS: St. 1, traditional; sts. 2-3, Bert Polman
MUSIC: Traditional
Words © 1994 CRC Publications

- Add instruments:
  Handchimes or Orff instruments: F and C

  Glockenspiel: Play the melody.

  Finger Cymbals, Triangle, Jingles:

  Hand Drum, Claves, Tambourine, Wood Block:

For the Beauty of the Earth

13

1. For the ___ beau-ty of the earth, for the glo-ry
2. For the ___ beau-ty of each hour of the day and
3. For the ___ joy of ear and eye, for the heart and
4. For the ___ joy of hu-man love, broth-er, sis-ter,
5. For thy ___ church, that ev-er-more lift-eth ho-ly
6. For thy-self, best Gift Di-vine, to the world so

of the skies, for the ___ love which from our birth
of the night, hill and ___ vale, and tree and flower,
mind's de-light, for the ___ mys-tic har-mo-ny
par-ent, child, friends on ___ earth and friends a-bove,
hands a-bove, of-fering ___ up on ev-ery shore
free-ly giv-en, for that ___ great, great love of thine,

Refrain

o-ver and a-round us lies; Lord of all, to
sun and moon, and stars of light; Lord of all, to
link-ing sense to sound and sight; Lord of all, to
for all gen-tle thoughts and mild; *Christ, our God, to
her pure sac-ri-fice of love;
peace on earth and joy in heaven:

thee we raise this our hymn of grate-ful praise.
thee we raise this our sac-ri-fice of praise.

For Holy Communion

WORDS: Folliot S. Pierpoint
MUSIC: Conrad Kocher; arr. by W. H. Monk

Bells/Glockenspiels

Rev. Pierpoint wrote this text on a beautiful spring day, observing God's Creation near Bath, England. The hymn is offered to the praise of God and lists many reasons for praise.

This is one of the few texts and tunes shared by most major denominations in the United States. All children should be taught this hymn of faith.

Identify the form of the melody. How many phrases or complete musical ideas are there? (Three.) Are the phrases long or short? (Very long.) Is each phrase different or do you hear repetition? (Repetition.) What is the form? (AAB)

A line dance (similar to the Bunny Hop) works well to engage singers in this hymn. Use the half note as the unit of movement. Begin in a single file line, one person in front of the other. Each child should place his or her hands on the shoulders of the person in front of them.

Measures	Movement
1, 3, 5, 7	Right heel, left heel
2, 4, 6, 8	Hop, hop, hop (wait)
9 and 10	Grasp hands with the person in front and behind and form a circle
11 and 12	Move to the center and end with a yell

Stanzas 1, 2, 5 and 6 are sung as examples on the *FaithSongs* CD.

Other Ideas:
- Try the instrumental accompaniment below.
- The refrain makes an ideal spoken or sung antiphon (response) to any litany of thanksgiving or series of spoken thoughts concerning thankfulness.
- Ask the children to list the reasons for praise found in this hymn text and then to begin adding new ones of their own.

(JH)

God Is So Good

This classic praise song about God's care and providence is well known.

The chorus melody is easily taught by rote to your singers if they do not already know it. For older singers, this is an easily understood example of melodic sequence.

A new, more difficult melody has been added to make this "fresh" for new generations. Teach the second melody by first speaking the text in the rhythm of the tune. This is a patter tune. Patter tunes are fun to sing because they contain so many words and syllables.

The easier familiar tune should be sung in a *legato* manner (smooth) to contrast with the faster, more agitated countermelody (*agitato*).

Transfer the idea of *legato* and *agitato* to movement. The familiar *legato* tune can become a "sliding" movement, best done in socks (no shoes). The *agitato* tune can become a tiptoeing movement, with short steps like dancing on hot coals.

Other Ideas:

• Ask children to relate their "best of times" and "worst of times," either verbally or in writing. Respect the privacy of family matters and caution them about revealing incidents or occasions that might embarrass or upset others. Talk about how God can help in those difficult times.

• In the world after 9/11/01, children are well aware that bad things happen. Help them to use this song to understand that God is with them "through the good and through the bad."

(JH)

Anthem Setting: "God Is So Good" by John D. Horman (Abingdon Press 0687044073). General anthem for two-part treble voices and keyboard.

WORDS: Traditional, descant by John D. Horman
MUSIC: Traditional, descant by John D. Horman
Descant © 2003 Abingdon Press, admin. by The Copyright Co., Nashville, TN 37212

How Majestic Is Your Name

15

O Lord, _ our Lord, _ how ma-jes-tic is your name _ in all ____ the _

earth. O Lord, _ our Lord, _ how ma-jes-tic is your name _ in all ____ the _

earth. O _ Lord, _____ we praise your

name. O _ Lord, _____ we mag-ni-fy _ your

name: _ Prince of Peace, _ might-y God; O _ Lord _ God Al-

might - y. _____ O

WORDS: Michael W. Smith (based on Psalm 8:1, Isaiah 9:6)
MUSIC: Michael W. Smith
© 1981 Meadowgreen Music Company/ASCAP. All rights admin. by EMI Christian Music Publishing.

Praising God • Giving Thanks and Praise

It is important that young singers understand that the words they are singing are from the Bible. Read Psalm 8:1, 9 and Isaiah 9:6 from different translations. Find the texts in the song.

To help the children's rhythm listening skills, echo-clap rhythms made up of quarter notes/rests and eighth notes/rests. Start with one-measure rhythms in 4/4 time. (Use the same tempo as the song.)

Move to two-measure rhythms choosing any two measures in the chart below. End with the rhythm found in measures 9-10 in the keyboard part, treble clef. The singers can clap this rhythm during these measures as well as in measures 13-14 and 21-22.

Other Ideas:
• Simple percussion parts can be added: tambourine, drum, claves.
• Be careful to keep a steady tempo. The excitement of this song can cause the tempo to speed out of control.

(KE)

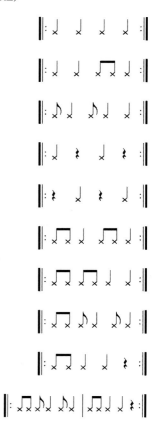

Acts 4 tells of Peter and Paul as they faced criticism and prison for teaching about Jesus. These two men were told to stop preaching, but they respond by saying that they "cannot keep from speaking about what we have seen and heard" (Acts 4:20). Read stanza 3 of this anthem to see how our composer uses Acts 4:24-30 to proclaim God's sovereignty.

Discuss how we can share about Jesus when we face criticism. Have the children identify places and situations where they felt pressure to avoid sharing about Jesus. Ask them how they could have responded.

The eighth-note pulse is of importance. Create a chart showing the relationship of the note values in this song.

Create a rhythm chart as shown.

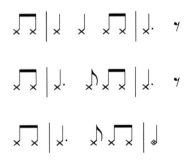

Define the note values as to the number of eighth notes or pulses that make up that note. Clap or play the patterns using rhythm instruments. These three rhythms are used throughout.

God of Mercy, God of Grace

16

1. God of mer - cy, God of grace, show the brightness of your face. Shine up - on us, Sav - ior, shine, fill our hearts with light di - vine, and your

(2. Let your) peo - ple praise you, Lord; be by all that live a - dored. Let the na - tions shout and sing glo - ry to their Sav - ior King; let all

(3. Sov-'reign) Lord, who made the earth, you have giv - en us new birth. Grant your ser - vants speak your Word, and with bold - ness call you Lord. While you

WORDS: Sts. 1 & 2, Henry Francis Lyte, alt.; st. 3, Joe Cox (based on Acts 4:24-30)
MUSIC: Joe Cox

Praising God • Giving Thanks and Praise

Chant-sing stanza 1 on an F, observing the rhythm as written. Echo to learn the pitches and text.

Other Ideas:
- Secure the cutoffs on the dotted quarter notes by pulsing them three times before the final consonant. Add snaps on the consonants to place them correctly.
- Sing as a call to worship or general anthem.
- Stanza 3 may be used as a call to worship for Communion or as a general benediction.

(GW)

What joy rises in our spirits as we approach God in worship! The Psalms are filled with songs of praise and glad hearts before the Lord. Think about these words as you enter worship next week. Is your heart filled with gladness? Do your songs bring praise to God? Read what the psalmist writes in Psalm 100. Can you find verses that match words in this song? Also read Psalm 118:24. What did you discover?

Echo-sing the refrain. Can the singers find the two phrases that sound the same? (Measures 9-10 and 13-14.) Which two phrases sound similar but end differently? (Measures 11-12 and 15-16.) The refrain is a question and answer. Measures 9-12 ask a musical question. Ask the singers if they hear that it sounds unfinished. Measures 13-16 are the answer. Do you hear how it completes the musical thought?

Other Ideas:
- Add instruments (tambourine, wood block, claves) on this pattern:

- Add instruments (maracas, guiro, cabasa) on this pattern:

- Sing this fun song during the opening of informal gatherings, such as Sunday school, choir, vacation Bible school, or camp. It may be used as a call to worship.
- The refrain may serve as an antiphon for either Psalm 100 or Psalm 118.
- To create a longer anthem, repeat the song several times or simply repeat the last phrase. The example on the *FaithSongs* CD repeats the final phrase as a possible extended ending.

(GW)

He Has Made Me Glad

WORDS: Leona Von Brethorst
MUSIC: Leona Von Brethorst

Praising God • Giving Thanks and Praise

In times of trouble and fear, the psalmist called to God for help. In Psalm 18, the writer is praising God for safety from an enemy. Help your children to see the "enemy" in anything that would harm their relationship with or displease God.

When the singers are comfortable with the stanza melody, try to sing the canon in the first seven measures. This can be a leader/group format or two equal groups. Remember to extend the last note of each phrase so that the harmony is evident.

This vivacious melody calls for movement that glorifies and exalts God. At the refrain, have the group form a circle (or circles) and join hands.

1. Circle right for eight counts (quarter note counts).
2. Walk in for four counts.
3. Back out for four counts.
4. Circle left for eight counts.
5. Walk in for four counts.
6. Back out for four counts.
7. Lift hands in praise for four counts.

Try doing this with colorful parachutes, scarves, or streamers. What a colorful way to praise God as the parachutes, scarves, or streamers circle, walk in, back out, and lift in exaltation!

(KE)

I Will Call upon the Lord

WORDS: Michael O'Shields (based on Psalm 18:2-3)
MUSIC: Michael O'Shields
© 1994 Universal-MCA Music Publishing (a div. of Universal Studios, Inc.) and Sound III, Inc.

Praising God • Giving Thanks and Praise

The tune HYMN TO JOY was composed by Ludwig van Beethoven (1770–1827) for the final movement of his Symphony No. 9. The applause that followed the first performance went unnoticed by the composer because of his total deafness. A member of the chorus turned Beethoven around to face the audience and receive their admiration.

This is one of the texts and tunes shared by all major denominations in the United States. All children should be taught this hymn of faith.

With the exception of one lower D, there are only five tones used in this melody, making it one that many children can pick out on the piano.

Without telling them what is about to be played, ask if anyone can "name that tune" and then play the first three pitches of the melody. Add one pitch at a time until the tune is named. Ask if anyone can play it all the way through.

Other Ideas:
• Younger children will love using this hymn like a marching song, with many percussion instruments.
• Assign the middle two stanzas as spoken solos. After singing the first stanza, insert the two solos and follow them with a short interlude, using the last line of the accompaniment. Then sing the last stanza to close.
• Learn more about Beethoven's life. His early life studying music and his later life composing while coping with the loss of hearing can be inspiring to children.

(JH)

Joyful, Joyful, We Adore Thee

WORDS: Henry Van Dyke; st. 4, alt.
MUSIC: Ludwig van Beethoven; arr. by Edward Hodges

Praising God • Giving Thanks and Praise

Make a Joyful Noise unto the Lord

The opening phrase uses an ascending five-note scale. The second phrase uses a descending five-tone scale. Teach the melodic movement on the body.

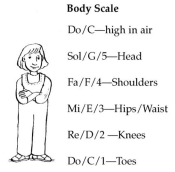

Body Scale

Do/C—high in air

Sol/G/5—Head

Fa/F/4—Shoulders

Mi/E/3—Hips/Waist

Re/D/2—Knees

Do/C/1—Toes

Begin by singing the tones on solfège syllables or numbers as you move up and down the five-note scale. Add the text and rhythm from the song.

When you know the melody line and text and have mastered all the intervals, it is time to add the handchimes or resonator bells. Consider teaching the instrument part by using the body scale.

Other Ideas:
- Try singing the song as a two- or three-part canon.
- Devise simple percussion parts.
- Use the first four measures as an antiphon for Psalm 66 or 100. Sing the entire song at the conclusion of the psalm.

(KE)

*May be sung as a three-part round.
**May use voices or rhythm instruments.
***Cued notes may be sung last time.

WORDS: Jimmy Owens
MUSIC: Jimmy Owens

Praising God • Giving Thanks and Praise

This song closely resembles Psalm 150 with its inventory of instruments used to praise God. Read Psalm 150 and list each instrument named. What instruments are named in this song? Natalie Sleeth, the writer and composer of this song, names other ways to praise the Lord. Can you and your singers find them?

Echo-sing measures 1-7. Note the ascending melodic pattern in measures 1, 3, and 5. Sing these measures, illustrating the repeating melodic pattern. Can your singers find this pattern elsewhere in the music? (Measures 9-15 and 25-31.) Sing these sections.

Teach measures 17-24. Point out that the pattern from measure 1 is turned upside down in these measures (17, 19, and 21).

Label the musical form: A A B A

Other Ideas:
- Add instruments on the half note pulse (tambourine and finger cymbals).
- Add a C instrument on the melody (flute or recorder).
- Sing as a round.
- Sing this as a general anthem of praise or call to worship. It may be used as a gathering song for Sunday school.
- Extract the final section of stanza 1, measure 25 through beat 2 of measure 31, as an antiphon for Psalm 150 or other praise psalm.

(GW)

Praise the Lord with the Sound of Trumpet

21

May be sung as a canon.

WORDS: Natalie Sleeth
MUSIC: Natalie Sleeth
© 1976 Hinshaw Music, Inc. Used with permission.

Praising God • Giving Thanks and Praise

18 Am Dm Gm C7 F F7

wind and sun - shine, praise the Lord in the dark of night,
time of sor - row, praise the Lord in the time of joy,

21 Bb Gm C Am Dm Gm7

praise the Lord in the rain or snow or in the morn - ing
praise the Lord ev - ery mo - ment; noth - ing let your praise de -

24 C F Dm Gm C

light. Praise the Lord in the deep - est val - ley,
stroy. Praise the Lord in the peace and qui - et,

27 F Dm Gm C Am Dm7

praise the Lord on the high - est hill, praise the Lord; nev - er
praise the Lord in your work or play, praise the Lord ev - ery -

30 Gm F Bb C 1 F Am Bb C 2 F

let your voice _ be still.
where in ev - ery   way!

Praising God • Giving Thanks and Praise

Our primary purpose is to offer praise to God. When we sing "Alleluia," a form of the Hebrew word *Hallelujah,* we are saying "all of you praise the Lord."

Echo-sing measures 1-4. These two repeated phrases will be easy to teach. Note the ascending and descending contour of the melody. Identify the dotted eighth/sixteenth rhythm of the first two notes. Can your singers find this pattern in other measures?

Sing the stanza as a call and response. You sing measures 1 and 3; the children respond on measures 2 and 4. Variations: Children sing the call and the director sings the response; divide the choir into two groups with one on the call and the other on the response; or sing as written.

The stanza is in D minor and the refrain is in D major. Discuss the different sounds of major and minor tonality. Try singing the refrain in D minor (use F naturals). How does it change the sound? How does it make you feel?

Other Ideas:
• Add instruments with the refrain as noted below the score.
• Sing this as a general anthem or offertory in worship during Easter or Pentecost.
• Stanza 1 may be used as a general call to worship. Stanza 2 may be used as a response for baptism or confirmation. Stanza 3 may be used as an introduction or response to the offering.

(GW)

Sing Alleluia

1. Peo - ple all come sing and shout; God is in us dwell - ing.
2. Ev - ery one a child of God, sis - ter or a broth - er.
3. For the gifts that we re - ceive, come with thank - ful giv - ing.

Spread the joy - ful news a - bout; sing with voic - es swell - ing.
All who know the love of God, share with one an - oth - er.
Let the prom - ise we be - lieve light the life we're liv - ing.

Refrain

Sing al - le - lu - ia, sing al - le - lu - ia;

raise your voic - es, shout with joy; sing praise to God, the Sav - ior.

Orff Instruments

Tambourine

Hand Drum

Alto Glockenspiel

Finger Cymbals

Soprano Metallophone

WORDS: Sue Ellen Page; revised 1986 Eric D. Johnson
MUSIC: Sue Ellen Page
© 1968, rev. 1986 Choristers Guild

Praising God • Giving Thanks and Praise

The Heavens Are Telling

The heav-ens are tell-ing the glo-ry of God; _ The
earth God's won-ders dis-play. _ They si-lent-ly show _ all God's
mar-vel-ous works _ to the whole world night _ and day. _
I will sing prais-es to you, O _ Lord; Sing
prais-es to your ho-ly name. _ I will sing prais-es to
you, O Lord; your glo-ry I will ev-er pro-claim. _____

Psalm 19 opens with this universal declaration of the glory of God. All bear witness to the mighty wonders of God. Throughout Creation, we can see God's handiwork displayed.

Melodic and rhythmic repetition makes this easy to teach. Echo-clap and speak the words in half phrases. Divide the choir into two groups. Group 1 claps and speaks the first half phrases; group 2 claps and speaks the next half phrases. Continue this process, working through the song.

Ask the singers to find each rhythmic pattern of four eighth notes. Speak the text each time this pattern is used.

Other Ideas:
- Add simple arm movements to help visually interpret the song such as moving one arm up (measure 1), then the other (measure 2), and then making a circle as the arms move back down to the singers' sides (measures 3-4.) Continue to improvise movements for the remainder of the text using the same movement pattern for each phrase; one movement for the first measure, another movement for the second measure, and a slower/longer movement during the last two measures of a phrase. Remember to consider the space available as you develop the movements.
- Sing as a general praise song in Sunday school or similar gathering. Use as a call to worship or as an antiphon to Psalm 19.

(GW)

WORDS: Linda Rebuck (based on Psalm 19)
MUSIC: Tom Fettke

Praising God • Giving Thanks and Praise

Sing to the Lord

This song combines the excitement of dance with a traditional Hebrew melody. Imagine the joy of the Hebrew children as they worshiped God after crossing the Red Sea.

Partner songs are an easy approach to two-part singing. Teach each part as a separate melody. Once the parts are sung confidently, divide the choir into two equal groups. Appoint a leader for each group, then combine the two parts.

Other Ideas:
- Performance options: Younger singers can sing the melody and older singers the descant. Use men/adults on the melody and boys/children on the descant.
- Read the conclusion of the Exodus story (Exod. 14:21-31; 15:1-21). View the end of the animated movie, *Prince of Egypt*.
- Teach the grapevine step or the hora dance to your choir. Devise a simple circle dance (move to the right, left, center, out).
- Tie colorful ribbons to a tambourine or wooden embroidery hoop. Imagine Miriam dancing with her timbrel as you move with the ribbons.

(GW)

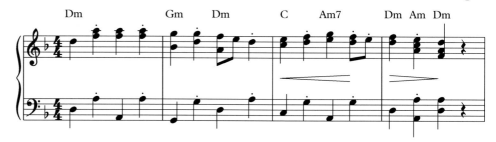

Anthem Setting: "Sing to the Lord" arranged by Liz Rose and David L. Bone (Abingdon Press, 063906). Unison and piano, optional two-part and obbligato instrument.

WORDS: Liz Rose and David L. Bone
MUSIC: Traditional Hebrew melody; arr. by Liz Rose and David L. Bone
© 1996, 1999 Abingdon Press, admin. by The Copyright Co., Nashville, TN 37212

This traditional Caribbean tune offers many opportunities for improvisation. You may invite the children to add stanzas or notes over the melody. Instrumental parts may also be improvised in addition to the ones suggested below.

Halleluja is a Hebrew word meaning "praise (ye) Jehovah." It may be spoken as a word of exclamation or sung as a hymn or song of praise.

Identify and clap the syncopation in the first two measures and similar phrases of the refrain. For fun, have the children stand quickly when they sing the syncopation, then return immediately to their seats.

Repetition is the best teacher for this song. Invite the singers to clap or use other body percussion while the leader sings. They will soon be joining in on the words.

Other Ideas:
• Add instruments:

Shaker (maracas, cabasa):

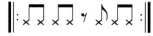

Hand drum, congas, or bongos:

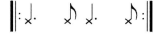

Claves or wood block:

• Sing as a general anthem of praise or as a gathering song.
• Invite the congregation to sing the refrain and to join in on the "hallelujas" at the end of each stanza.
• The refrain may be used as a call to worship.

(GW)

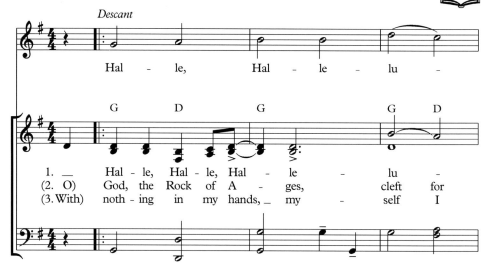

WORDS: Trad. Caribbean; stanzas 2, 3, Augustus M. Toplady, adapt.
MUSIC: Trad. Caribbean, arr. by Hal H. Hopson, adapt.; descant by David L. Bone

He Came Down

This tune is from the Cameroon tradition. Cameroon is a republic in western Africa. Triangular in shape, this country lies close to the equator and remains warm and rainy year-round.

Use the spoken phrase, "Tune from Ca-me-roon" to pick up the prominent rhythm from the odd-numbered measures of the song.

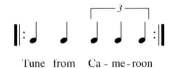

As in other African music, simple movement is appropriate—a gentle swaying from side to side can be very effective. Also, a right foot, left touch, left foot, right touch motion is in keeping with the tradition.

Other Ideas:

- Choose a different percussion instrument to play for each word: love, peace, and joy. Play the instrument on the rest that follows the word when it occurs in the song.
- A stanza of this song can be sung each week during the lighting of the Advent wreath. Create additional stanzas using single syllable theme words you are using in your Advent and Christmas celebration. Adding a stanza with each passing week will complete the song on Christmas Eve.
- The song can be used with any other words: grace, hope, life, light, and so on.

(JH)

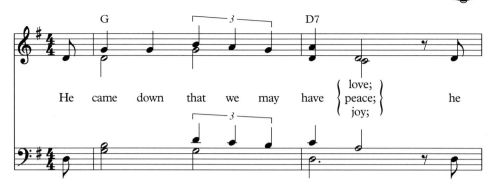

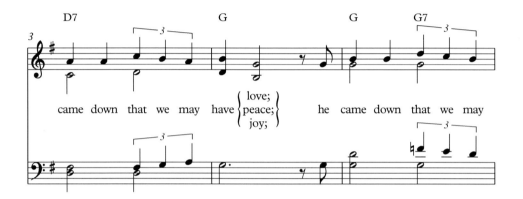

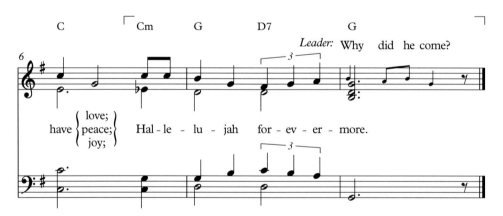

WORDS: Trad. Cameroon
MUSIC: Trad. Cameroon; transcribed and arr. by John Bell

Praising God • Giving Thanks and Praise

I Love You, Lord

The text of the song expresses several ways of loving God: telling God "I love you, Lord"; lifting one's voice in song and praise; worshiping; and rejoicing. We hope that our acts of worship and the way in which we live our lives will please God and bring God joy.

Because the tempo is relatively slow and each musical phrase is four measures long, deep breathing and breath control are musts. Practice a variety of breathing exercises, such as "breathing air in through a straw" and breathing in for four counts, holding for eight, and breathing out for four. Strive for a pure, gentle vocal tone that is supported by deep breaths and good singing posture.

Show the children when to say the "ss" sound of "voice" and "rejoice" (on beat 3). Tap the beat on thighs and snap when the "ss" occurs. Urge them to say the "ss" together and to minimize the sound.

Other Ideas:
- The singers could sing alone the first time through and then invite the congregation to join them on the repeat(s).
- For accompaniment, consider keyboard and/or guitar, or add a worship band.
- To add a visual element to the song, sign the text or develop a simple, fluid dance, which could be performed by soloist or a small group. (See page 6 for a list of sign language resources.)

(NB)

WORDS: Laurie Klein
MUSIC: Laurie Klein

Praising God • Giving Thanks and Praise

Jesus, Jesus, Let Us Tell You

Jesus sent his Spirit to dwell among us so that we would not be alone. It is by his Spirit that we find comfort, peace, and guidance in our daily life. It is by his Spirit that we are confident in the Resurrection of our Lord.

Echo-sing two-measure phrases with the children. While you sing, use the sign for "Jesus" and tap the half note pulse in alternating hands to keep a steady beat.

When the children are confident singing the melody, add the piano playing the melody in canon with the singers. Next, invite the singers to sing in canon.

Other Ideas:

- Sing on Pentecost or when the great commandments scriptures are used.
- Textually, this song is related to "Love God with Your Heart" (page 64) and "Luke 10:27" (page 66).
- Add a guitar (preferably an electric) in a pseudo-reggae rhythm, playing G minor on beats 1 and 2 and D minor on beats 3 and 4. Ad lib and include additional chord changes. Use percussion instruments and/or worship band as desired.
- Encourage the children to write their own verses.

(GW/NB)

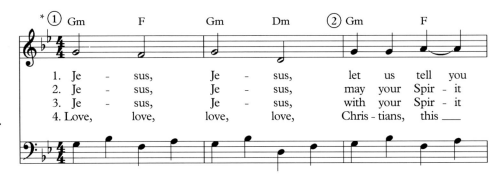
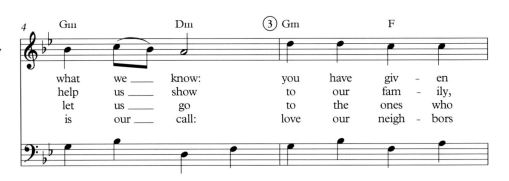
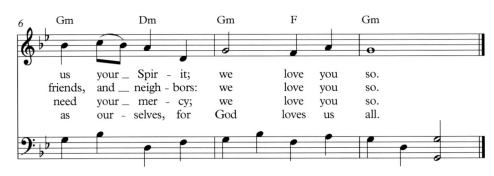

1. Je - sus, Je - sus, let us tell you
2. Je - sus, Je - sus, may your Spir - it
3. Je - sus, Je - sus, with your Spir - it
4. Love, love, love, love, Chris - tians, this ___

what we ___ know: you have giv - en
help us ___ show to our fam - ily,
let us ___ go to the ones who
is our ___ call: love our neigh - bors

us your ___ Spir - it; we love you so.
friends, and ___ neigh - bors: we love you so.
need your ___ mer - cy; we love you so.
as our - selves, for God loves us all.

May be sung as a round.

WORDS: Sts. 1 & 4, Traditional; st. 2, Bert Polman; st. 3, Joanne Hamilton
MUSIC: Traditional; arr. by Richard L. Van Oss
Sts. 2 and 3 and arr. © 1994 CRC Publications

Jesus

Praising God • Giving Thanks and Praise

O For a Thousand Tongues to Sing

1. O for a thou - sand tongues to sing my
2. My gra - cious Mas - ter and my God, as -
3. Je - sus! the name that charms our fears, that
4. He speaks, and listen - ing to his voice, new

great Re - deem - er's praise, the glo - ries of my
sist me to pro - claim, to spread through all the
bids our sor - rows cease; 'tis mu - sic in the
life the dead re - ceive; the mourn - ful, bro - ken

God and King, the ___ tri - umphs of his grace!
earth a - broad the ___ hon - ors of thy name.
sin - ner's ears, 'tis ___ life, and health, and peace.
hearts re - joice, the ___ hum - ble poor be - lieve.

WORDS: Charles Wesley
MUSIC: Carl G. Gläser; arr. by Lowell Mason

This hymn text was written by Charles Wesley to celebrate the one-year anniversary of his spiritual conversion. During a conversation with Peter Bohler, a Moravian friend, Wesley asked him about praising Christ. Bohler replied, "Had I a thousand tongues, I would praise him with them all." This was Wesley's inspiration for the text.

This is a text and tune shared by all major denominations in the United States. All children should be taught this hymn of faith.

This hymn uses notes of only three different durational lengths—the eighth note, the quarter note, and the half note. Try singing the tune through using these words: RUN for eighth notes; WALK for quarter notes; SLIDE for half notes.

Phrase 1: WALK– RUN–RUN– WALK–WALK–RUN– RUN–WALK–WALK – RUN–RUN–WALK– WALK–SLIDE.

Can the children change these words to movement while listening to the hymn?

For a fun percussion accompaniment, assign the following instruments to the three note values:

Eighth notes: Maracas
Quarter notes: Drums
Half notes: Tambourines

Other Ideas:
- Sing with strength and a firm tone, in a marchlike manner.
- Encourage the children to learn more about Charles Wesley.
- A simple dotted half-note "Al-le-lu-ia!" vocal descant on high D and C (measure 6) makes this short hymn a lovely and appropriate introit for service use when the children sing for morning worship.

(JH)

Discuss the acts of redemption/salvation expressed in the song: "You came from heaven to earth to show the way," "from the earth to the cross my debt to pay," "from the cross to the grave," "from the grave to the sky."

Echo-sing and tap (put two fingers of one hand in the palm of the other hand) the song in two-measure phrases. Strive for clear, clean rhythms. Help the children see/hear that the notes and rhythms of the following measures are identical: measures 1-2 and 5-6; and measures 3-4 and 7-8. Measures 9-10 and 11-12 are similar, and measures 13-14 are built upon a repeated rhythmic pattern.

Sing with crisp diction and a lot of energy. When deciding on a tempo for the song, consider the wordiness of measures 9-16. Choose a tempo that comfortably accommodates the text of these measures.

Other Ideas:

- Because it is a song of praise, "Lord, I Lift Your Name on High" is especially appropriate during the opening part of a worship service or assembly.
- If your church has a worship band (keyboard, guitars, and drums), invite the members to accompany the song. Be sure the volume of the instruments doesn't cover up the children's voices.
- Encourage your group to create a rhythmic clap pattern for measures 2, 4, 6, 8, and 16 to add even more excitement.

(NB)

Lord, I Lift Your Name on High

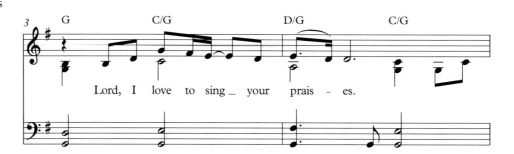

WORDS: Rick Founds
MUSIC: Rick Founds

Praising God • Giving Thanks and Praise

No Other Name

Sign language and movement will enhance the melody and the text of this piece. Be very comfortable with the signing and the phrasing before adding the movement.

Form a large circle and have the singers face into the center while signing and singing the first ten measures.

Measure 11:
Holding hands, all slowly raise hands over head.

Measure 12:
Pulse raised hands upward and to the RIGHT twice on the half note pulse.

Measure 13:
Pulse raised hands upward and to the LEFT twice on the half note pulse.

Measure 14:
Slowly lower hands.

Measures 15-16:
Walk in for eight counts; slowly lift hands.

Measures 17-18:
Back out for eight counts; slowly lower hands.

Repeat the first ten measures with sign language and singing.

Sign Language: NO, OTHER, NAME, JESUS, LORD, WORTHY, GLORY, HONOR, POWER, PRAISE

Other Ideas:
• Help the children use a Bible concordance to make a list of some of the names for Jesus found in the Bible.
• Consider asking a soloist to sing measures 11-18 as in the example on the *FaithSongs* CD.

(KE)

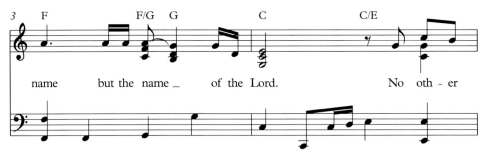

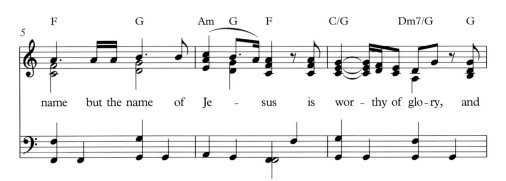

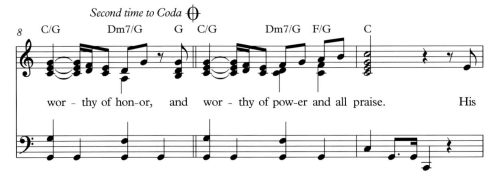

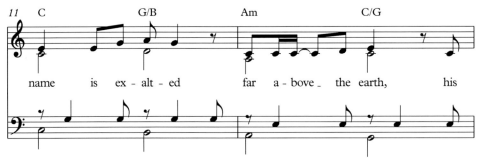

WORDS: Robert Gay
MUSIC: Robert Gay
© 1988 Integrity's Hosanna! Music (ASCAP) c/o Integrity Media, Inc., 1000 Cody Road, Mobile, AL 36695.

Praising God • Giving Thanks and Praise

name is high a-bove the heav-ens. ___ His

name is ex-alt-ed far a-bove the earth, give

D.S. al Coda

glo-ry and hon-or and prais-es to his name. No oth-er

⊕ CODA

wor — thy of pow — er and all praise.

No

Other

Name

Jesus

Lord

Worthy

Glory

Honor

Power

Praise

Praise the Lord, All Creation

Children will love this exuberant praise song. The claps add rhythmic vitality and fun.

Echo-sing and tap two fingers of one hand in the palm of the other through measures 5-12 in two-measure phrases. When the rhythms are crisp and clean, sing the passage in its entirety. Repeat the procedure for measures 13-20.

Add the claps as indicated. Percussion instruments can reinforce the claps if desired. If the children are singing the song in worship, encourage the congregation to clap also.

This song works well with keyboard and guitar. The style of the piece also lends itself to a Caribbean feel. In this style, add guitar, drums, and Latin percussion instruments; use a steel drum, marimba, or xylophone patch on the MIDI keyboard; have the bass guitarist play the bass notes of the keyboard accompaniment or something similar (eliminate the left-hand part in the keyboard); and add an optional ad lib flute part.

Other Ideas:
- Use this song as a companion song with "The Trees of the Field" (page 94).
- Because it is a song of praise, this song is especially appropriate during the opening part of a worship service or assembly. It could be used as a call to worship, an act of praise, or as a response to the scripture.
- In addition to general use, it may be sung as part of Earth Day celebrations or on any day when God's world is the focus.

(NB)

Rhythm instruments may be used in addition to claps.

WORDS: Linda Rebuck
MUSIC: David Huntsinger and Bonnie Huntsinger

Praising God • Giving Thanks and Praise

15 Dm / G / C

Praise the King ___ of kings. ___ Praise _ the Lord, –
Praise the King ___ of kings. ___ All ___ the stars ___
Praise the King ___ of kings. ___ Wor - ship him, ___

18 F C / C/G G7 C | 1, 2

all cre - a - tion; *(clap, clap)* Praise the Lord. ___
in the heav - ens; *(clap, clap)* Praise the Lord. ___
all cre - a - tion; *(clap, clap)* Praise the Lord. _

21 | 3 Gsus G C

___ *(clap, clap)* Praise the Lord! *(clap, clap, clap)*

In his letter to the church at Philippi, Paul admonishes us to rejoice in all of life. Tell the children that Paul was in prison when he wrote these words. Ask them to imagine what Paul's life was like in prison and how he was able to find joy in his heart.

Read Philippians 4:4-7 and reflect on how we are to live. List on the board Paul's suggestions in this passage.

Teach the melody, then sing as a round (start the round at the pickup to measure 5.)

Choreograph movement:
1. Invite one circle to move around the circle or in/out of the circle (for example, walk to the right seven steps, then reverse).
2. Invite another circle to stand still and use body percussion (for example, patsch, clap, snap, clap).
3. All use movement 1 on the first two phrases. Use movement 2 on the second two phrases.

Create a circle for each canon group. Have group 1 begin singing with the movement. Group 2 begins singing and moving at the appropriate time, and so forth.

Other Ideas:
• Use the Orff-style accompaniment instead of the piano accompaniment.

Rejoice in the Lord Always

34

WORDS: Evelyn Tarner (based on Philippians 4:4)
MUSIC: Evelyn Tarner

Praising God • Giving Thanks and Praise

gain I say re - joice! Re - gain I say re - joice!

Bb C F   Bb C F

Metallophone

• This song may be used in worship as a response to the Philippians 4 passage.

(GW)

📖 35

Heleluyan

**He - le - lu - yan, he - le - lu - yan. __ He - le, he - le - lu - yan.
Hal - le - lu - jah, hal - le - lu - jah. __ Hal - le, hal - le - lu - jah.

He - le - lu - yan, he - le - lu - yan. __ He - le, he - le - lu - yan.
Hal - le - lu - jah, hal - le - lu - jah. __ Hal - le, hal - le - lu - jah.

*May be sung as a round.
**Pronounced: hay-lay-loo-yahn

WORDS: Traditional Muskogee (Creek) Indian
MUSIC: Traditional Muskogee (Creek) Indian, transcribed by Charles Webb
Transcription © 1989 The United Methodist Publishing House, admin. by The Copyright Co., Nashville, TN 37212

Other Ideas:
• Consider giving each of the children a chance to play the drum. If you have several drums, encourage your older children to accompany the group as everyone sings. Add jingle bells to the drum pulse.
• Use this song as a response to the reading of the Gospel. Use the alternate text during a worship service centered on the gift of music.

(DT)

This song is thought to have originated just prior to or during the Trail of Tears, a forced walk of the Creek and Cherokee peoples to Indian Territory (what is now the state of Oklahoma) during the dreadful cold winter of 1838–1839.

The hymn has been kept alive through oral tradition for over one hundred years and was first published in *The United Methodist Hymnal* in 1989. This makes the written form of this song just a few years older than your singers.

Using a hand drum playing on the quarter note pulse, sing the song to the children. Ask the children to join you as you move in a circle, stepping on the beat.

Tell them that this song was taught by oral tradition and that some Muskogee (Creek) peoples sing the first phrase with different words. Sing the first phrase, substituting "Yah-hay-ka-thei" ("I will be singing") for "Heleluyan" in the second measure. You may want to let the children decide which text they would like to sing together.

Shine, Jesus, Shine

Because the text invites God's Spirit among us, this song is especially appropriate during the opening part of a worship service or assembly. In addition to general use, the song is suitable for Advent, Epiphany, Lent, Christ the King, and any other time when the image of "light shining in the darkness" is used.

The song can be sung in a variety of ways: for example, in a broad tempo (as a majestic praise song), or as an upbeat, energetic song. The upbeat tempo works well with children; however, be sure to set the tempo based on how fast they can comfortably sing the verse, *not* the refrain.

Consider creating motions for the refrain. Ask one of the children who takes dance lessons to create the motions for you.

Other Ideas:

• For an intergenerational approach, invite the children to sing the refrain and the verse alone, with youth and/or adults joining on the following refrain. (If additional choirs and/or congregation are used, you might consider having brass play on the refrain.)

• If your church has a worship band, invite the band to accompany the song. Check sound levels so the instruments and voices are balanced.

(NB)

WORDS: Graham Kendrick
MUSIC: Graham Kendrick; arr. by Jack Schrader, adapt.
© 1987, arr. © 1998 Make Way Music, admin. by Music Services in the Western Hemisphere

Praising God • Giving Thanks and Praise

Lord, the light of your love is shin - ing

in the midst of the dark - ness shin - ing;

Je - sus, Light of the World shine up - on ___ us,

set us free by the truth you now bring ___ us. Shine on ___

me, shine on ___ me.

Shout to the Lord

As you are learning this song, begin a collection of pictures that show the majesty of God's Creation and the beauty of the earth. The words need companion images of the magnificence of God's beautiful world.

Sing at a fairly slow tempo so that all the words can be understood. The syncopated rhythms will be easily grasped by the singers if you sing them clearly and correctly the first time. Echo-sing two-measure phrases.

Ask the choir to silently lip-synch with either the recording or your singing. Look for active mouths. This will help not only in memorization, but also in text declamation. Ask one half of the group to sing while the other half mirrors them and lip-synchs.

Other Ideas:
- Make a banner that depicts the wonder of God's Creation and the magnitude of God's promise to us. Display the banner for the congregation when your group sings this song.
- One way to learn this text is by encouraging the children to interpret it visually. Create several learning centers. Display the artwork when the children share this song in worship.
  CLAY CENTER: Have the children create clay sculptures to depict the text.
  MOVEMENT CENTER: Using the CD, ask a team to create movements for the group.
  ART GALLERY: Use small scraps of construction paper and glue to create paper mosaics that represent the text.

(KE)

WORDS: Darlene Zschech
MUSIC: Darlene Zschech

Praising God • Giving Thanks and Praise

Noth-ing com-pares _ to the prom - ise I have _ in _

you.

you.

Optional extended ending: Repeat measures 13 and 14 three times before singing "in you" the final time.

With My Whole Heart

The simplicity of this prayer reminds us of our need to dedicate our whole being to the Lord, not just a part. We are simply asked to put nothing above our love and praise of Christ and to give him the service of our heart, mind, and life.

The melodic line is appropriate for young singers as well as older elementary students. Be sure to explore the interval of the descending fifth (5-1, sol-do, A-D), which is found several times in the song. Ask the children to touch their shoulders and then their knees each time they sing this interval.

Other Ideas:

• Create motions for the song. As the singers become familiar with the movements, encourage them to follow the phrasing of the music with extended, graceful movements. You may also want to ask someone to teach sign language to the text.

• Use this song as preparation for or as a response to prayer. Consider using this song as a part of an adult baptism or a confirmation liturgy. At other times in the Christian Year, it would be appropriate for a Lent, Advent, or mission emphasis.

• Cut out large paper hearts and ask the children to write a short note or a prayer on the heart. Send the hearts to some of your homebound members.

(KE)

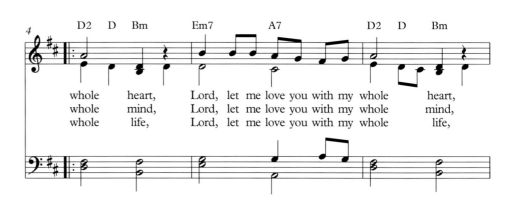

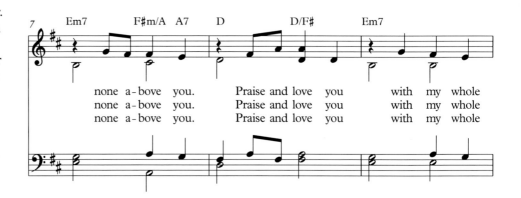

WORDS: Kenny Wood
MUSIC: Billy Crockett

Praising God • Giving Thanks and Praise

Lord, let me hear you with my whole heart, ev-er near you.
Lord, let me hear you with my whole mind, ev-er near you.
Lord, let me hear you with my whole life, ev-er near you.

Help me hear you with my whole heart.
Help me hear you with my whole mind.
Help me hear you with my whole

2. With my
3. With my

life. _____

The singing of "gloria" is offered as an act of praise. We see this phrase uttered at the end of the Epistles as a thankful greeting between believers. We also hear the angels singing it at the birth of Christ.

This song also praises God, Jesus, and the Holy Spirit—the Trinity. Some congregations call this response the Gloria Patri. Do you sing these or similar words in worship? Help the children to explore the similarities and differences in several trinitarian songs.

You may recognize this melody with other words, "Michael, Row Your Boat Ashore." The melody is easily accompanied on the autoharp. Have everyone imitate strumming an autoharp on the half note pulse as they sing this melody. Invite various children to accompany the choir on the autoharp as all imitate the strum.

Other Ideas:

• Add handbells or choir chimes. Assign bells in the three chords to three groups of singers (D = D, F#, A; G = G, B, D; A, A7 = A, C#, E, G). Use flash cards with the chord names to help the ringers know when to change the chords.

• Sing this as a general praise song in an informal setting such as Sunday school, vacation Bible school, or camp.

• It may be used in worship as the Gloria following the creed, assurance of pardon, Gospel lesson, or as appropriate to your congregation.

• Stanza 1 may be used as a call to worship during Christmas. Stanza 2 may be used on Trinity Sunday.

(GW)

Glory Be to God on High

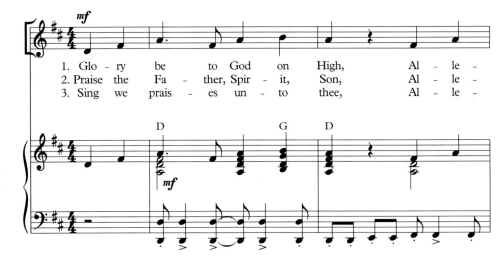

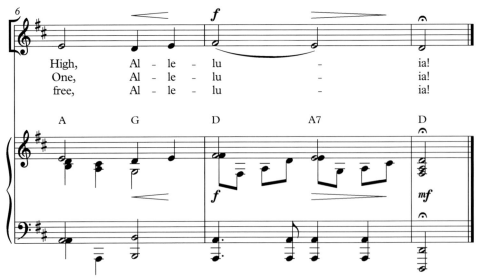

WORDS: Traditional
MUSIC: Traditional, arr. by John D. Horman
Arr. © 2003 Abingdon Press, admin. by The Copyright Co., Nashville, TN 37212

Praising God • Giving Thanks and Praise

¡Miren Qué Bueno!
(O Look and Wonder)

Refrain*

¡Mi - ren qué bue - no, qué bue - no es! es!
O look and won - der, how good it is! is!

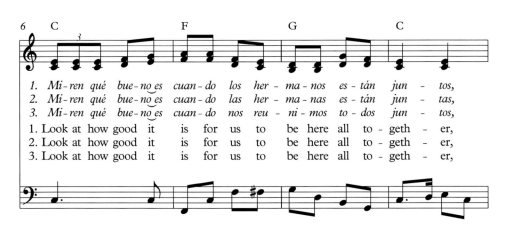

1. Mi - ren qué bue-no es cuan-do los her - ma-nos es - tán jun - tos,
2. Mi - ren qué bue-no es cuan-do las her - ma-nas es - tán jun - tas,
3. Mi - ren qué bue-no es cuan-do nos reu - ni-mos to-dos jun - tos,

1. Look at how good it is for us to be here all to - geth - er,
2. Look at how good it is for us to be here all to - geth - er,
3. Look at how good it is for us to be here all to - geth - er,

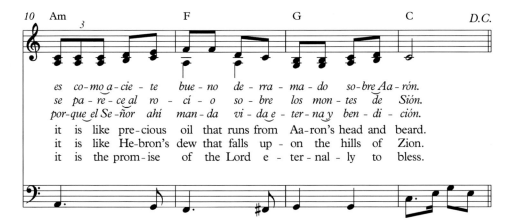

es co-mo a-cie - te bue - no de - rra - ma-do so-bre Aa - rón.
se pa - re-ce al ro - cí - o so - bre los mon - tes de Sión.
por-que el Se - ñor ahí man - da vi-da e - ter-na y ben - di - ción.

it is like pre-cious oil that runs from Aa-ron's head and beard.
it is like He-bron's dew that falls up - on the hills of Zion.
it is the prom-ise of the Lord e - ter-nal - ly to bless.

*Refrain is repeated each time.

WORDS: Pablo Sosa; English trans. by George Lockwood (based on Psalm 133)
MUSIC: Pablo Sosa
© 1979 Concionero Abierto; trans. © 1996 Abingdon Press, admin. by The Copyright Co., Nashville, TN 37212

Ask a child to read Psalm 133. Share with them that in Bible times pouring oil over a person's head was a symbol of joy or hospitality and that the reference to Aaron reminds us that pouring of oil was also a part of the ordination of priests. The image of dew is that of the delight of moisture coming into dry lands.

Spanish Pronunciation Guide:
MEE-rehn kay BWEH-no,
kay BWEH-no EHS.

Teach your singers this hand pattern for the refrain, moving to the quarter note pulse:
• Tap your knees two times.
• Clap your own hands two times.
• Clap your partner's hands two times.
• Clap your own hands two times.
• Repeat all.
Ask them to find a partner and try to sing and tap/clap the refrain together. Tell the children to find a new partner as you sing the stanzas. The children should join as they sing and tap/clap on the refrain.

Other Ideas:
• Some of the children may want to write their own stanzas about times of joy in their own life. Ask them to fill in the blank: "Being together with you at church makes me feel as happy as the time I _____."
• Consider asking the congregation to sing the refrain during the Passing of the Peace. As a leader or the choir sings the stanzas, the congregation greets one another in the name of Christ.
• Consider adding claves, playing the rhythm of the melody line in the first measure.
• Your children and congregation will enjoy singing the refrain in Spanish, like the example on the *FaithSongs* CD.

(DT)

Be Still and Know

Discuss what it means to "be still and know" who God is. This will be a foreign concept to many children, whose lives overflow with bustling activity. Ask them to remember times in their life when they have been still, such as being read to while resting in a parent's arms.

Using the text of the song as a point of departure, enable the singers to be quiet and to focus on God. Lead them in guided meditation, perhaps focusing on a lighted candle or closing eyes and concentrating on breathing in and out.

Ask the children what "I am the Lord who heals your life" might mean. Talk about the many ways God works to bring about healing in our lives. Also discuss what it means to "put our trust" in God.

While singing, raise and lower one hand to indicate the rise and fall of the melody.

Other Ideas:

- Use this as a prayer song during your choir rehearsals or Sunday school classes.
- This song can be used as a companion song with "When I Am Afraid" (page 169).
- Works well with guitar alone or with guitar and keyboard.
- To break up the stanzas, add an instrumental verse after verse 2, with flute or recorder playing the melody an octave higher than written. The wind instrument could ad lib on the last verse, perhaps playing the lower part of the treble keyboard line up an octave.
- Use a "Scale Ladder" to visually show the rise and fall of the pitches of the melody. See "Other Ideas" on page 9 for directions.

(NB)

WORDS: Anon., based on Psalm 46:10; Exodus 15:26; Psalm 31:14
MUSIC: Anon., arr. by David L. Bone
Arr. © 2003 Abingdon Press, admin. by The Copyright Co., Nashville, TN 37212

Hine Ma Tov

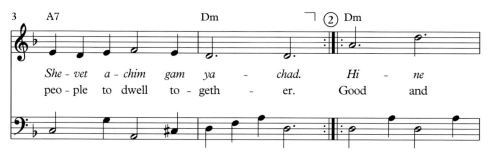

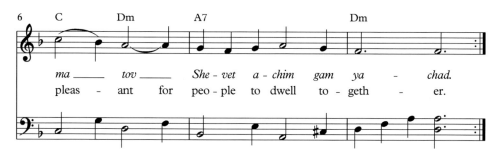

*May be sung as a two-part round.

WORDS: Psalm 133:1
MUSIC: Israeli round
Arr. © 1989 Graded Press, admin. by The Copyright Co., Nashville, TN 37212

• Add instruments:

Autoharp: Use chords in score.

Tambourine:

Triangle and/or finger cymbals:

Bass xylophone:

The psalmist knows the beauty of peace, whether between siblings, neighbors, or throughout the world. Read Psalm 133 and look at the metaphors for peace. Lead a discussion of past and present world leaders. Identify national figures as well as persons in your state or city. Discuss how the children can also be peacemakers.

Hebrew Pronunciation Guide:
HEE-neh mah tov oo-mah NA-yeem SHEH-veht a-HEEM gam YA-hahd.

The 6/4 meter feels as if it has two large beats in each measure. Play a dotted half pulse on a hand drum as you teach this melody. You may have the children clap, walk, or sway the pulse as they sing.

Add movement. Stand in a circle holding hands and facing clockwise.

Phrase 1: Walk eight steps around the circle on the dotted half pulse.
Repeat: Walk eight steps counterclockwise.
Phrase 2: Release hands, raise and lower arms gradually while turning to the left in place over two measures. Facing center, step–touch, step–touch to the left.
Repeat: Repeat, but step–touch, step–touch to the right.

Other Ideas:
• Sing as a round. Each group forms a different circle for the dance.
• Sing at general gatherings, such as Sunday school, VBS, and church camp.
• Sing the first phrase as an antiphon to Psalm 133. Sing the entire song as a response to scripture on peace.

(GW)

In Brazil, the music and cultures of immigrants as well as native persons have greatly influenced each other. African and Latin American rhythms merge together to form new patterns. The text, inspired by Psalm 98, is in Portuguese.

Portuguese Pronunciation Guide:

Kahn-TAH-ee ah-oo Seh-ÑOR oom KAHN-tee-koh NOH-voh

(*ñ* is pronounced like the *gn* in "lasagna")

Ask the children to draw the shape of the melody in the air as it is played. Help them to discover that the melody begins at a high point and then descends several times in the song. Share with them that this is typical of this vocal tradition.

Sing the song to the children using the text. Ask them to listen for the words "Cantai ao Senhor." How is the melody for those words different from the rest of the phrase? (In each four-measure phrase, the first half moves by skips; the second half moves mainly by steps and repeated notes.)

If you are using the *FaithSongs* CD, the first stanza is sung in Portuguese, followed by stanzas 1, 4, and 5, which are sung in English.

Other Ideas:

• Teach the internal beats of each measure as strong–weak–weak. Patsch–snap–snap each measure. Add a sway with the body, left then right, once per measure to group the hand pattern into measures.

• Ask an instrumentalist to improvise a flowing countermelody to play after the children know the melody.

Cantai ao Senhor
(Rejoice in the Lord)

WORDS: Psalm 98, para. by C. Michael Hawn
MUSIC: Brazilian folk melody; arr. Simei Monteiro
Paraphrase © 1999 Choristers Guild. Arrangement © Simei Monteiro, administered by Choristers Guild.

Praising God • God's Word

• This waltz tune should be felt in ONE rather than THREE, accompanied by keyboard and guitar. A recorder or flute could be used to teach the melody to the children.

(DT)

Come Bless the Lord

This song uses two verses of Psalm 134, telling us to bless or praise the Lord. This psalm is last in a group of psalms that travelers used on their way to the Temple in Jerusalem (Psalms 120–134).

Ask the children, "Why do you think the travelers wanted to bless the Lord?" (Safe travel, opportunity to worship, and so on.) Verse 3 of the psalm sent the travelers out with a benediction: "May the LORD, maker of heaven and earth, bless you from Zion." Remind the children that we also gather to praise and bless God and are sent out with God's blessing.

Play this teaching game with the children. Echo-chant and clap the text to each phrase. Sing the song, asking the children to continue to clap the text rhythm after you sing each phrase.

Alternate groups—those who sing the phrase and those who clap the response—switching back and forth until the melody is secure.

The echo has a melody that is sometimes different from the main melody. Ask the group to sing the main melody as you sing the echo. Do this several times, adding children to the echo until the group is divided evenly.

Play the game again, making circles in the air with the pointer fingers on the longer notes.

Other Ideas:
- Sing this song at the opening or closing of your rehearsal or class session.
- Use this as a call to worship or gathering or as a benediction response in worship. Teach the congregation the main melody, with the children singing the echo.

(DT)

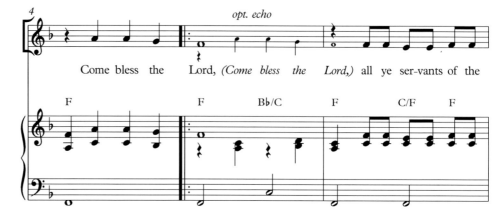

WORDS: Psalm 134:1-2
MUSIC: Traditional

Praising God • God's Word

hands *(Lift up your hands)* in the ho - ly place, *(in the ho - ly*

place,) and bless the Lord, *(and bless the Lord,)* and bless the

Lord. *(and bless the Lord.)* Come bless the Lord.)

Love God with Your Heart

In Matthew 22:36-40 and Mark 12:29-31, Jesus was quoting the Jewish declaration of faith, the *Shema* (shuh-MAH). The first portion of this ancient prayer is found in Deuteronomy 6:4-9. The Shema is placed in a box at the door of Jewish homes so that each person who enters is reminded of the importance of loving God with all that they are.

Divide the singers into three groups. Teach each group one of the four-measure phrases. Sing the phrases in sequence. Next, try to stack the three phrases. Have the first group repeat their phrase over and over, then add the second phrase group. When these two are secure, add the third phrase group. Now your singers are ready to sing in three-part canon.

Other Ideas:
- This song works well with guitar, arpeggiating the chords rather than strumming.
- Use the song as a vehicle for teaching the minor scale, the interval of a perfect 4th down (G to D), and the octave (D to D).
- Sign the following words:
    LOVE, GOD, HEART, NEIGHBOR, YOURSELF
    LOVE, GOD, MIND, NEIGHBOR, YOURSELF
    LOVE, GOD, STRENGTH, NEIGHBOR, YOURSELF
- "Luke 10:27" will make an interesting companion song (see page 66). The text is essentially the same, but the musical styles are very different. The final stanza of "Jesus, Jesus, Let Us Tell You" is also based on this scripture (page 40).

(NB)

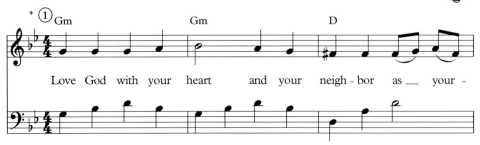
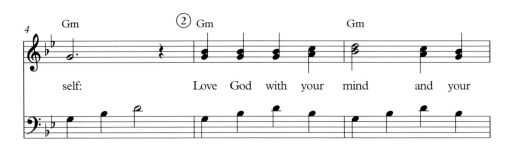

Love God with your heart and your neigh-bor as __ your-self: Love God with your mind and your neigh-bor as __ your-self: Love God with your strength and __ your __ neigh-bor as your-self.

May be sung as a three-part round.

WORDS: Mark 12:30-31, adapted
MUSIC: Traditional folk melody; arr. by David L. Bone
Arr. © 2003 Abingdon Press, admin. by The Copyright Co., Nashville, TN 37212

Love   God   Heart   Neighbor   Yourself

Mind   Strength

Praise the Lord

WORDS: Deut. 6:5-6; adapt. by Debi Tyree
MUSIC: Japanese koto melody; arr. by Nylea L. Butler-Moore

Adapt. © 2003, arr. © 1993 Abingdon Press, admin. by The Copyright Co., Nashville, TN 37212

Praising God • God's Word

In its original form this Japanese tune is called "Sakura" and was written to carry a text about the beauty and tranquility of cherry blossoms in springtime. Many of your singers may have learned this version in their school music program.

This is a song of quiet contemplation. Sing it with a *legato* sound (tones connected with as few breaths as possible). Sing at a slower than usual tempo and maintain a mood of thoughtfulness and serenity.

The dance below will help set this mood. It is best done with slow, smooth movements. Begin with both knees on the floor, head bowed, and hands folded as if in prayer.

Measure Number	Movement
1	Lift head.
2	Slowly rise to a standing position.
3	Raise right arm with outstretched hand, fingers extended.
4	Raise left arm and outstretched hand, fingers extended.
5-6	Lower elbows to waist level. Cross hands on chest.
7-8	Move hands out at chest level, make fists on the word "might."
9-10	Open hands and slowly lower arms to sides.
11-12	Same as 3 and 4.
13-14	Slowly kneel, fold hands, and bow head.

Other Ideas:
• Use light percussion: triangle, finger cymbals, and so on. Choose key words with the children and highlight those words with these instruments.
• Add a flute on the melody.
• Use this question as a theme: How do we give praise to God? What other songs of praise do you know? How is this song different from those songs? (It is quiet and calm.)

(JH)

The parable of the Good Samaritan is very familiar to children. This parable was used by Jesus to expound on the ancient Hebrew teaching that is quoted in Luke 10:27. Combine this song with a study of this parable.

Many "contemporary" songs contain a lot of syncopation; "Luke 10:27" is no exception. Practice speaking the text in rhythm through ending 1, while tapping the beat on thighs. Help the children feel that many of the notes "bounce off the beat"; they are syncopated. When the rhythms are precise, add the pitches. Repeat the procedure for ending 2.

Ask a child to play a simple tambourine part (for example, shake–hit–shake–hit). Add shakers and other percussion instruments on the repeat.

Other Ideas:

• Ask the singers to create a pantomime of the parable of the Good Samaritan. Alternate portions of the pantomime with portions of this song. Accompaniment can continue during the pantomime. End with the final section, "Do this and you will live."

• Use the song in conjunction with a mission activity or as a theme song. Encourage the children to choose an activity that shows their love for God and neighbor.

• This is a great upbeat song to use with a worship band. Just be sure that the instruments don't drown out the children's voices.

• "Love God with Your Heart" would make an interesting companion song (see page 64). The text is essentially the same, but the musical styles are very different. Stanza 4 of "Jesus, Jesus, Let Us Tell You" is also based on the same text (page 40).

WORDS: Luke 10:27-28
MUSIC: Roger Day; arr. by David L. Bone
Music and arr. © 2000 Roger Day

- Make word charts with the words YOU, LOVE, LORD, GOD, HEART, SOUL, STRENGTH, MIND, NEIGHBOR, and YOURSELF.
- Make a game out of holding up the word charts. Scramble the charts and have the children put the words in correct order. Play "surprise!" Hand out charts to the children but tell them not to let anyone know what their word is until they hold up their sign.
- Use sign language with the words on the charts (see page 64).

(NB)

This song was written in 1971 following a Bible study on the scripture from which it is derived (Matt. 6:33; 7:7). Shared informally, the song soon became a favorite and was included in early collections of Contemporary Christian music. This is one of the first songs from this movement to make it into the mainstream of worship music. It is now included in the hymnals of many denominations.

Learn to sign the following words as a lead-in to learning the song:

SEEK: Make the letter "C" with palm facing left; circle several times in front of face.

ASK: Place open hands palm to palm in front of chest; draw them toward the body.

FIND: Place open hand in front of you, palm down; draw thumb and forefinger together; lift as if you are picking something up.

KNOCK: Make a fist; pretend to knock on an imaginary door in front of you.

OPEN: Hold both hands in front at chest level, palms facing outward and side by side. Draw hands apart like two sliding doors opening.

RIGHTEOUS: Make the letter "R" with your right hand, push it from wrist to fingertips of the palm of the left hand (palm up).

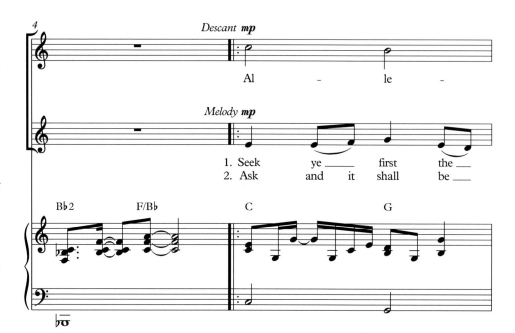

WORDS: Karen Lafferty; descant by Karen Lafferty (based on Matthew 6:33; 7:7)
MUSIC: Karen Lafferty

Praising God • God's Word

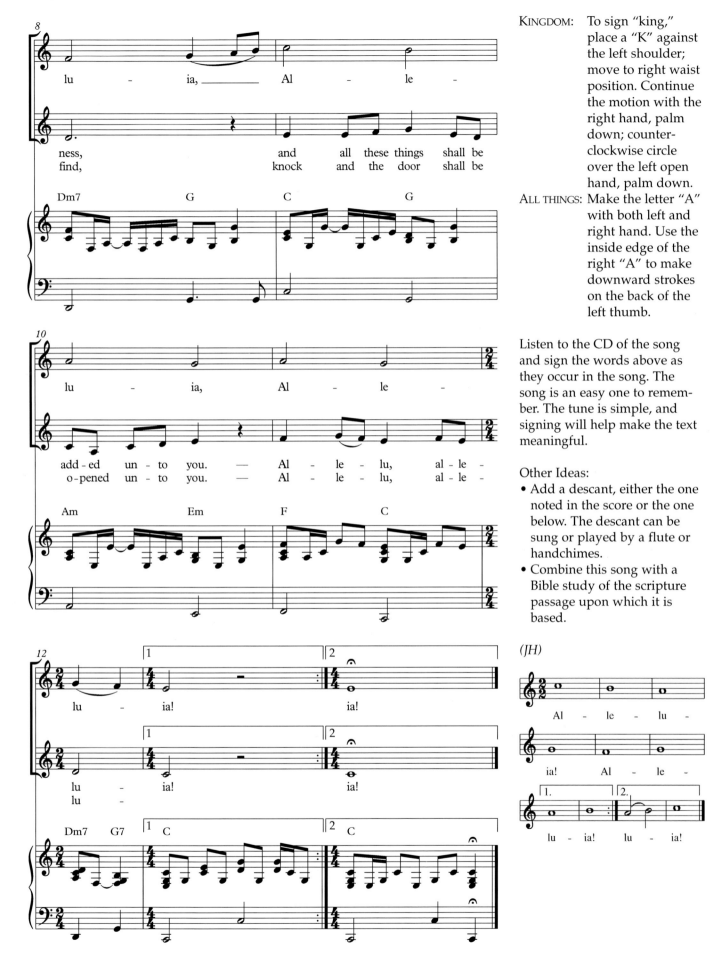

This is a song that requires only two chords to accompany. To prepare the children to play the F chord (F-A-C) and the C7 chord (C-E-G-B♭) in the correct places, ask them to listen to the melody while an F chord is played on the piano. Instruct them to raise their hand when the chord sounds "wrong." Tell them that is where the C7 chord belongs. Figure out the correct sequence or arrangement of chords by listening.

Write the chord sequence on either a chalkboard or chart paper (F-F-C7-F). Add the two chords on autoharp or handchimes. The pattern will repeat four times to complete the song.

Join hands and create a circle. Walk to the right on the first phrase of the song, then walk to the left on the second phrase. On the third phrase, raise arms and move to the center of the circle, then back out again on phrase 4. Once the song is learned, it can be sung and danced as a canon using two circles. The first circle starts alone, followed by the second circle at the halfway point in the song. Singing the song twice makes the dance more effective and enjoyable.

Other Ideas:
• Sing this beautiful psalm setting when reading or studying Psalm 23. It is also a good song to sing when discussing the Old Testament concept of "shepherding" or the ongoing care and protection of God.
• Using the signs for "shepherd" and "always" will help the children better understand the concepts.

(JH)

The Lord Is My Shepherd

WORDS: Traditional (based on Psalm 23)
MUSIC: Traditional

50 Where Shall I Go from Your Spirit?

God's presence is all around us as evidenced in Psalm 139. Read this Psalm, or verses 7-10, which correspond to the song. Tell the children "God is everywhere and no matter where we go, God is there."

This song is based on the E♭ major scale. Create a scale pattern on the board or on a poster using scale numbers or solfège. Illustrate the A section melody, measures 1-15, by pointing to the corresponding pitches. Echo-sing each phrase. You may use this process for the B section, measures 16-33.

The B section range is an opportunity to work on beautiful singing tones. Use the melody as a vocal warm-up; sing on nonsense syllables, such as "loo." Illustrate good posture and breathing for singing. Demonstrate a tall, open sound.

Create variations on this melody to keep the exercise fresh. Vary the rhythms, tempo, dynamics, and syllables. Use the body to illustrate the sound by moving the arms, walking, or dancing the phrase as you sing.

Other Ideas:
- The optional part 2 may be sung and/or played on a C instrument, such as flute or violin.
- Sing in worship as a response to Psalm 139 or a similar psalm.
- The A section may be sung alone as an antiphon or as a song.
- Sing as an anthem in response to a sermon on God's presence.
- Use a "Scale Ladder" to visually show the rise and fall of the pitches of the melody. See "Other Ideas" on page 9 for directions.

(GW)

WORDS: Psalm 139:7-10
MUSIC: Kenney Potter
Music © 2001 Choristers Guild

Praising God • God's Word

When we pray, we are talking to God and we know that our prayers are heard and that God blesses us in many ways. This wonderful prayer song can be used in the worship service as a call to prayer or a response to prayer.

A simple side-to-side step/touch movement can be added as the children become comfortable with the gospel feel of this prayer. Once the children are comfortable with the step/touch movement, consider adding simple, *legato* arm movements also or sign the text.

Help the children work together on singing the final consonants together, especially on the words "Lord," "Spirit," "place," and "grace." Ask the children to snap as they sing the final consonant. Are they snapping together?

Other Ideas:
- Use this song in your choir rehearsal during a prayer time. Sing the song, then hum while a leader or child prays aloud.
- The descant can be added by using recorders, chimes, handbells, or a few voices.
- The example on the *FaithSongs* CD repeats the final phrase as a possible extended ending.

(KE)

Lord, Listen to Your Children Praying

Lord, lis-ten to your chil-dren pray - ing, _____

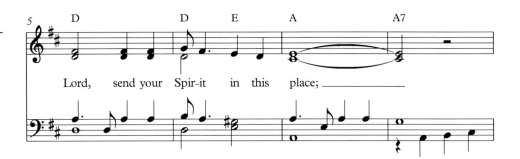

Lord, send your Spir-it in this place; _____

Lord, lis-ten to your chil-dren pray - ing, _____ send us

love, send us power, send us grace! _____

WORDS: Ken Medema
MUSIC: Ken Medema

O God in Heaven

1. O God in heav - en, _____ grant to thy chil - dren _____ mer - cy and bless - ing, _____ songs nev - er ceas - ing, _____ love to u - nite us, _____ grace to re - deem us, _____ O God in heav - en, _____ dear Lord, our God.

2. Je - sus, Re - deem - er, _____ may we re - mem - ber _____ thy gra - cious pas - sion, _____ thy res - ur - rec - tion. _____ Wor - ship we bring thee, _____ praise we shall sing thee, _____ Je - sus, Re - deem - er, _____ Je - sus, our Lord.

3. Spir - it de - scend - ing, _____ whose is the bless - ing, _____ strength for the wea - ry, _____ help for the need - y; _____ sealed in our kin - ship, _____ thine be our wor - ship, _____ Spir - it de - scend - ing, _____ Spir - it a - dored.

WORDS: Elena G. Maquiso; trans. by D. T. Niles
MUSIC: Elena G. Maquiso; harm. by Charles H. Webb

The text of "O God in Heaven" allows the children in your group to explore the Holy Trinity. Ask if they have ever heard someone say: "In the name of the Father, the Son, and the Holy Ghost."

Ask what parts of the Sunday morning service contain references to the Trinity (creeds, prayers, hymns, songs). Do they know any other songs or hymns that refer to the Trinity? ("Holy, Holy, Holy.") Use the shamrock as a way to remember the Trinity.

Share with them that this song was written by the composer/writer Elena Maquiso of the Philippines.

Introduce the song by playing the melody on a recorder or other C instrument, asking the children to hum with the melody. Help them to sing long *legato* phrases by moving a scarf or streamer in slow circles in front of the body, lifting the scarf up and down with each breath.

Other Ideas:
- Companion songs on the Trinity: "Come, Be Baptized" (page 82) and "Glory Be to God on High" (page 56).
- Add a simple percussion ensemble by assigning the following rhythmic patterns to the song:

  Claves: Beats 1 and 2
  Finger cymbal or triangle: Beat 3
  Drum: Beat 4

- Use the three stanzas individually as service music in worship or sing the entire hymn as an anthem.
- Use a solo C instrument as the introduction and for melodic support.

(DT)

In the Old Testament, the sanctuary was the place where God lived among the people. Because God's presence was there, it was a holy place. Only the high priest, the highest ranking religious leader, after much preparation, could enter the sanctuary.

The text of the song asks God to make us a "living sanctuary," that is, to make our lives a place where God lives. Just like the high priest of old, we are to be "pure and holy, tried and true." We should strive to be devoted to God, living lives of goodness that reflect God's presence.

Help the children correctly and clearly sing the sixteenth-note rhythms. Speak the rhythm of the song on "pah" while tapping the rhythm with two fingers in the palm of the other hand. Then sing on "pah" and tap the rhythm. When the rhythms are clean, add the words.

Create a chart like the one shown below. Using the quarter note as the point of reference, explain that two eighth notes equal one quarter note; four sixteenth notes equal one quarter note; two quarter notes equal one half note; and four quarters notes equal one whole note.

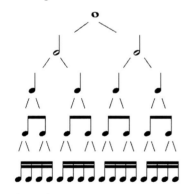

Other Ideas:
- The song is especially appropriate for use during the prayer time in rehearsals and worship.
- Works well with keyboard and/or guitar, or with a worship band.

(NB)

WORDS: John Thompson and Randy Scruggs
MUSIC: John Thompson and Randy Scruggs; arr. by Nylea L. Butler-Moore

Santo, Santo, Santo
(Holy, Holy, Holy)

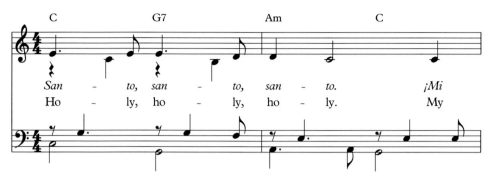

San - to, san - to, san - to. ¡Mi
Ho - ly, ho - ly, ho - ly. My

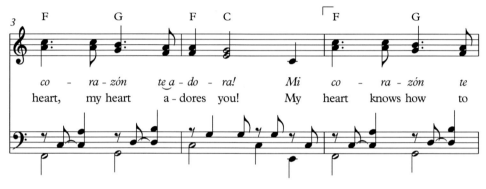

co - ra - zón te a - do - ra! Mi co - ra - zón te
heart, my heart a - dores you! My heart knows how to

sa - be de-cir: ¡San - to e - res, Dios!
say to _ you: You are ho - ly, Lord!

WORDS: Argentine folk song
MUSIC: Argentine folk song; arr. by Carlton R. Young
Arr. © 1995 General Board of Global Ministries, GBGMusik

Spanish Pronunciation Guide:
    SAHN-toh SAHN-toh SAHN-toh
    mee KOH-rah-sohn teh ah-DOH-rah
`   mee KOH-rah-sohn teh SAH-beh deh-SEER
    SAHN-toh EH-rehs DEE-ohs
    (The "r" sounds should be flipped.)

This beautiful chorus from Argentina puts into melody and words the feeling of deep love and awe that we have as we try to tell others of the holiness of God.

Introduce this song to the children using a recorder or flute to play the melody. Ask them to hum the melody the instrument is playing. As they become comfortable with the melody, begin to sing the text and encourage them to join you as they are able.

Consider teaching this in Spanish first, as the beauty of the melding of text and tune shines through in the original language. Move between the Spanish and English as you sing, and alternate with humming.

Other Ideas:
• Use this as an intercessory prayer song with the children during your time with them. Sing the song several times. As you hum together, lift up prayer concerns of your community. Then, as you finish the concerns, sing the song again, moving back to a hum and the prayer. Repeat this pattern several times. After several experiences with this model of prayer, the children will begin to offer their own prayers during the humming.
• Consider using guitar and recorder, flute, or violin when singing this as an anthem or with the congregation in worship. Create a gentle arpeggiated accompaniment pattern on the guitar. The recorder, flute, or violin can play the melody or improvise their own part.

(DT)

Children have a deeper understanding of faith and of commitment to God than we give them opportunities to express. This prayer song helps them put into words their desire to follow God and to be filled with God's love.

Introduce the song by having someone play it softly in the background, asking the children to follow you in these motions. Make the motions slow and graceful to match the *legato* style of the music.

Begin to hum the melody as you move and invite the children to join you. Once they are comfortable humming the melody, line out the song text phrase by phrase.

Other Ideas:
- The word "seal" refers to a promise made between God and you to love one another. This promise is sacred and is never to be broken. Ask the children about times they have made promises. How difficult is it to keep that promise? Share with them times of promise in your worship, such as during a baptism, confirmation, membership vows, and so on.
- Use this song as a response to prayer, or during a service of reaffirmation of the baptismal covenant.
- If times of silent prayer or contemplation or an altar call are part of your worship tradition, encourage the children to sing this song to themselves as a way to help them focus their thoughts.
- This would be especially appropriate for the children to sing on Ash Wednesday and during Lent.

(DT)

Take, O Take Me As I Am

55

WORDS: John Bell
MUSIC: John Bell

Motions
"Take O take"
    Close hands into fist at chest level; slowly stretch both arms out and move them up toward the sky, while opening fists. Eyes and head should follow this movement.
"Summon out"
    Slowly move alternate hands from the heart to the sky.
"Set your seal"
    Slowly cross hands and move them to the heart, slowly tapping the chest with crossed hands.
"And live"
    Move arms and hands to the side and slowly bring them up in front of the body, moving beyond the head to reach up high. Eyes and head should follow hands.

Praising God • Prayer

Doxology
Word Scramble

REIPAS   ODG   MFOR   OWMH   LAL   SGIBNSLES   WOLF;

____ __ ____ ____ __ _____ ____;

REIPAS   MHI   LAL   ARTECERUS   RHEE   WELBO;

____ ___ ___ _____ ____ _____;

REIPAS   MHI   BVEAO   EY   VALEYNEH   SOTH;

____ ___ _____ __ _____ ____;

REIPAS   ETAHRF,   ONS   NDA   OLYH   OGTSH.   MENA.

____ _____, ___ ___ ____ _____ ____.

This song reminds us that monetary gifts are not the only things we should offer to God. The weekly offering is a regular part of our worship liturgy and often includes the singing of a doxology, or words of praise.

Teach the first eight measures to the children. Sing the entire song, inviting them to sing these measures while you sing the second half of the song. Soon they will be ready to sing the entire song with you.

Learn to sing the Doxology at the end of the song. If your congregation uses another setting, learn to sing it, too. You may want to substitute it for the one printed here.

Other Ideas:

• Ask the children: "When is the Doxology sung in our worship service?" "Whom are we praising in this song?" "Can you name all three images that are used for God?" (Father, Son, and Holy Spirit.)

• Sing this song during the annual stewardship campaign as an anthem or as the congregation brings their pledge cards forward.

• Use as an anthem for a community thanksgiving service or as an offertory anthem for general worship (the ushers return the offering plates as the Doxology is sung with the congregation).

• See the anthem setting for a simple handbell part.

(GW)

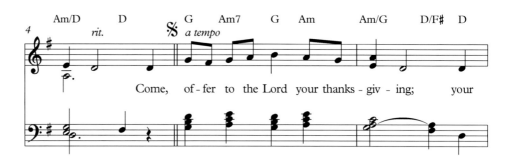

*for Communion Sundays

Anthem Setting: "Offertory Song" by Hal H. Hopson (Abingdon Press, 074401). Unison with keyboard and optional handbells and congregation.

WORDS: Hal H. Hopson; based on the Doxology text by Thomas Ken
MUSIC: Hal H. Hopson; based on OLD 100th
© 1994, 1998 Abingdon Press, admin. by The Copyright Co., Nashville, TN 37212

Praising God • Offering

time and strength,
love each day, } and try God's work to do. Come,
bread and wine,

CODA

sing. Praise God, from whom all

bless-ings flow; praise him, all crea-tures

here be-low; praise him a-bove, ye heaven-ly

hosts; praise Fa-ther, Son, and Ho-ly

Ghost.

Praising God • Offering

81

Come, Be Baptized

While the method of baptism may differ from church to church, the words are very similar: "I baptize you in the name of the Father, of the Son, and of the Holy Spirit." The text to this song is easy to memorize once you have helped the children remember this phrase, which they may have heard in worship.

They may also have heard "Father, Son, and Holy Ghost" in the text of the Gloria Patri if this is used in your worship service.

When teaching this song to the children, work with them to create beautiful vowel sounds, especially on the longer note values, such as on the diphthong "i" (AH+ee) in "baptized" or "a" (EH+ee) in "name."

If the children are having difficulty singing the text together in rhythm, ask them to sing the melody on a *staccato* syllable, such as "bop." They have to work together to make the rhythms exact. This song is also a good opportunity to help the children sing long *legato* phrases, while keeping the rhythms secure.

The stanzas to "Come, Be Baptized" can be found in *The Faith We Sing*, published by Abingdon Press.

Other Ideas:
- Learn the signs for the three parts of the Trinity.
- Use this song as an invitation to baptism as the family of the person to be baptized moves to the font.
- Consider using guitar and piano together as accompaniment, singing the chorus several times. Begin singing softly and get stronger on each repeat.

(DT)

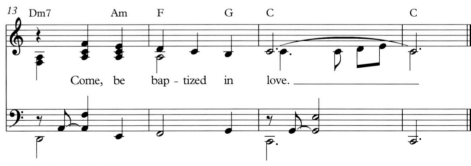

WORDS: Gary Alan Smith
MUSIC: Gary Alan Smith; arr. by Jack Schrader, alt.

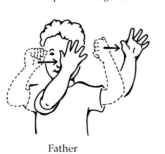

Father

Son

Spirit

Praising God • Baptism

Wonder of Wonders

59

1. Won-der of won-ders here — re-vealed;
2. Here in this sac-ra-ment — we see
3. This child of God, — though young — or old,
4. Now we our vow — of faith — re-new,

God's cov-e-nant — with us — is sealed.
God's grace un-bound, — for all, — for me!
we wel-come now — in to — Christ's fold,
stretch wide our sights — to glob-al view,

And long be-fore we know or pray,
May we re-spond with joy-ful praise
to know with us God's lov-ing care;
and claim with Chris-tians far and near

God's love en-folds us ev-ery day.
in lov-ing ser-vice all — our days.
here all our joys and sor-rows share.
a larg-er fam-i-ly — held dear.

Use a hand drum to intro-duce the lilt of the 6/8 meter by playing a quarter note/eighth note pattern as you hum the melody line. Sway gently in time to the music, encouraging the children to join you.

You may want to move about the room stepping time to the music and asking the children to follow you. If you can, continue this movement pattern and move together to the worship space. Lead them in singing the first stanza as they circle the font and then continue to hum and play the drum as you move back to your room.

Read the text of stanza 2 together. Ask a child to lead the group in playing the drum and sing the second stanza together. Give other children the oppor-tunity to play the drum as you read and sing stanzas 3 and 4 together.

Other Ideas:
- To create a slightly different accompaniment style, write a flute part. Consider asking a guitarist to play this with a moving eighth note pattern.
- To create an anthem arrange-ment with the guitar and flute, simply insert a short instrumental interlude (meas-ure 5 to the end) between the third and fourth stanzas.
- You may want to sing stanzas 1-3 prior to a baptism and stanza 4 after the baptism, in which case the interlude could also be played as the introduction to stanza 4 after the baptism.

(DT)

WORDS: Jane Parker Huber
MUSIC: *Katholisches Gesangbuch;* adapt. from *Metrical Psalter;* arr. by David L. Bone
Words © 1980 Jane Parker Huber. From *A Singing Faith.* Used by permission of Westminster John Knox Press.
Arr. © 2003 Abingdon Press, admin. by The Copyright Co., Nashville, TN 37212

Praising God • Baptism

Circle the Table

Combine this song with a study of Communion in your congregation. Discuss the institution of the Last Supper by reading Matthew 26:17-30; Mark 14:12-26; or Luke 22:7-23.

Experience the melodic lilt by adding movement. Patsch–snap–snap on the left side of the body, then repeat on the right side. Discuss the time signature and define each number.

Teach the rhythm pattern:

Locate examples in the music.

Other Ideas:
- See the anthem setting for liturgical dance suggestions.
- Sing in a Communion service as a general anthem, as the invitation to the table, or during the serving of the elements. It is especially appropriate for World Communion Sunday (first Sunday in October).
- Learn the Communion liturgy used in your church, memorizing the congregational responses. Assist in the preparation and serving of the elements on the day this song is offered in worship.

(GW)

Anthem Setting: "Circle the Table" by Mary Nelson Keithahn and John D. Horman (Abingdon Press, 337208). Unison and piano with optional descant or flute.

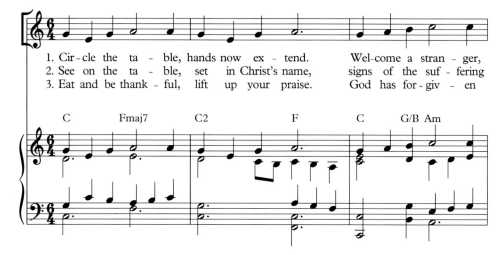

1. Cir - cle the ta - ble, hands now ex - tend. Wel-come a stran - ger,
2. See on the ta - ble, set in Christ's name, signs of the suf - fering
3. Eat and be thank - ful, lift up your praise. God has for - giv - en

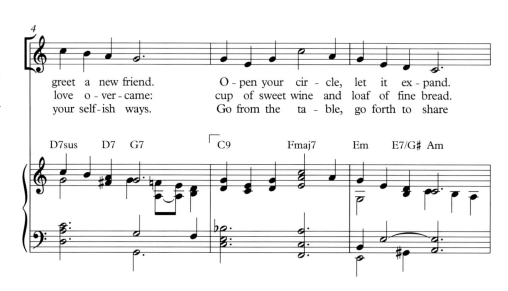

greet a new friend. O - pen your cir - cle, let it ex - pand.
love o - ver - came: cup of sweet wine and loaf of fine bread.
your self - ish ways. Go from the ta - ble, go forth to share

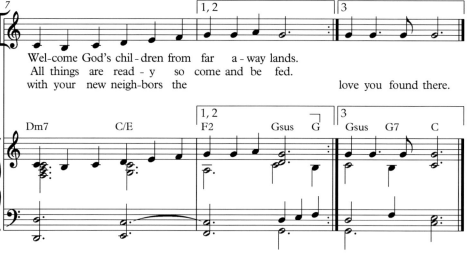

Wel-come God's chil - dren from far a - way lands.
All things are read - y so come and be fed.
with your new neigh-bors the love you found there.

WORDS: Mary Nelson Keithahn
MUSIC: John D. Horman

Jiu shi zhi shen
(The Bread of Life for All Is Broken)

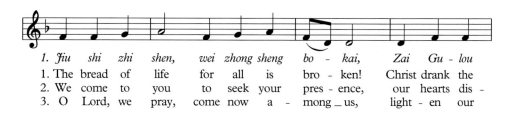

1. *Jiu shi zhi shen, wei zhong sheng bo-kai, Zai Gu-lou*
1. The bread of life for all is bro-ken! Christ drank the
2. We come to you to seek your pres-ence, our hearts dis-
3. O Lord, we pray, come now a - mong _ us, light - en our

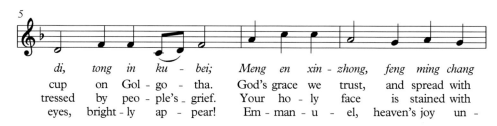

di, tong in ku-bei; Meng en xin-zhong, feng ming chang
cup on Gol-go-tha. God's grace we trust, and spread with
tressed by peo-ple's _ grief. Your ho-ly face is stained with
eyes, bright-ly ap-pear! Em-man-u-el, heaven's joy un-

ji - nian, Jing she sheng - yan, zhui - i _____ dang _ nian.
rev - erence this ho - ly feast, and thus re - mem - ber.
bit-ter tears; our hu-man pain you still bear with _ us.
end - ing, our life with yours for - ev - er blend - ing.

WORDS: Timothy Tingfang Lew; trans. by Walter Reginald Oxenham Taylor; phonetic transcription from
  the Chinese by I-to Loh; st. 2 & 3 adapted by David L. Bone and Debra R. Tyree
MUSIC: Su Yin-Lan

Phonetic transcription © 1989 The United Methodist Publishing House, admin. by The Copyright Co.,
Nashville, TN 37212

This hymn was published for the first time in 1936 in *Hymns of Universal Praise,* a hymnal used by the Protestant groups of China. I-to Loh, the phonetic translator of the text, notes that Walter Reginald Oxenham Taylor preserved the original meter of the text in his English translation. You will discover the beauty of this as you teach the song to the children.

Ask the children to say the text in English as they use their pointer finger to follow the melody line. Help them to discover that the rhythm of the melody and the English flow together.

Play the melody on a recorder or other instrument and ask the children to silently say the text as they listen. Echo-sing each phrase; repeat phrases as needed to help the children learn the text and melody.

The hymn is most haunting when sung unaccompanied or perhaps with a small gong or finger cymbals played as the half notes are held. A recorder or wooden flute could play the melody with the children. The tune can also be supported by playing a constant D and A below middle C on the organ or other pitched instruments.

Other Ideas:
- It is recommended that you ask a Chinese speaker to teach the phonetic transcription to the children.
- The individual stanza of this hymn works well as service music. Stanza 1 serves as a call to Holy Communion; stanza 2 can be used as a call to prayer or call to worship during Holy Week; and stanza 3 can be used as a call or response to prayer during Advent.
- If you are using the *FaithSongs* CD, two beats are added to the end of each stanza to allow for a good breath before the next stanza.

(DT)

Come to the Table of Love

The invitation to the table is a part of any Communion service. Some congregations use special words, called a liturgy, to begin Communion. Does your church follow a liturgy for this service? If so, study what these words mean. Invite your pastor to visit with your group and show you these words. Are they printed in your hymnal?

Clap the rhythm pattern of the first four sung measures. This rhythm appears three times in the music. Can your singers find all three? (Phrases 1, 2, and 4.) Sing each phrase and notice how the melodies are different.

The lilting nature of the triple meter lends itself to one pulse per measure. Invite your singers to stand in a circle and pretend to ice skate the dotted half pulse as the accompaniment is played. Feel the "swoosh" of each measure. Can they sing and skate at the same time? Try!

Other Ideas:
- Add sign language to help the children learn several of the key words of the text, such as COME, TABLE, LOVE, FAITH, HOPE.
- Sing in worship as an invitation to the Lord's Table; as the elements are presented or served; or as a general anthem for a Communion service.

(GW)

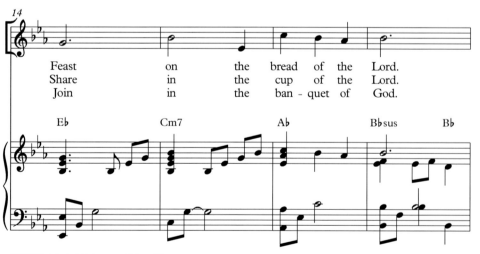

WORDS: Mark Friedman and Janet Vogt
MUSIC: Mark Friedman and Janet Vogt

Praising God • Communion

We are a fam - ily, one bod - y in Je - sus.
We are u - nit - ed, be - liev - ing in Je - sus.
We share to - geth - er one spir - it in Je - sus.

Come to the ta - ble of love.
Come to the ta - ble of faith.
Come to the ta - ble of

hope.

Come

Table

Love

Hope

Faith

As you teach this song to the children, keep a strong, steady beat. The fun of a melodic line that goes down by steps on eighth notes often takes over the steady beat and the singers will begin rushing the tempo.

Teach the first two phrases of the stanza and share that the melody they have just learned repeats for the second half of the stanza. Ask the children to sing the third and fourth phrases of the stanza to you. Play claves to help keep the beat steady. Work on enunciating the text clearly.

Ask the children to sit and tap their knees with their pointer fingers and listen as you sing the refrain. Ask them to say the text of the refrain in rhythm with you. Then sing the refrain together. Note that the refrain melody follows the same pattern as the stanza (two phrases repeated).

Other Ideas:
- Ask one group to sing measures 1-8, and the second group to sing measures 9-16. Join together on the refrain.
- Invite a person who speaks Spanish to share the pronunciation.
- Use guitar, maracas, and claves to accompany this song.
- Consider repeating the refrain several times, increasing the intensity each time. One way to do this is by asking the instruments to play simple rhythm patterns the first time you sing the refrain and gradually changing to more active rhythm patterns as you repeat the song or refrain.

(DT)

Canto de Esperanza
(Song of Hope)

WORDS: English St. 1 and refrain by Alvin Schutmaat
MUSIC: ARGENTINA Argentine folk melody, setting by Tom Mitchell
© 1993 Choristers Guild

Praising God • Sending Forth

Enviado Soy de Dios
(Sent Out in Jesus' Name)

The text to "Enviado Soy de Dios" reminds us of our call to create a new kingdom here on earth that is filled with love, justice, and peace. Children will especially enjoy the image of being able to do work that angels cannot do: "The task is ours to do."

Ask the singers to listen to the first two phrases of the song. Are they the same or different? (The same.) As you sing the phrase "to make the earth the place," show them the shape of the melody line by drawing on a board or having a poster drawn in advance. Ask how many other phrases in this song share the same shape of the melody line. (There are six more phrases with the same melodic pattern.)

Consider asking a person from Cuba to teach the children the pronunciation of the Spanish text.

Other Ideas:
- Create simple rhythmic patterns for maracas, hand drums, claves, and tambourine using the rhythm patterns found in the accompaniment.
- If you have a guitar player available in your setting, use the guitar and the rhythm instruments to accompany the children in worship.
- Consider adding hand claps on beats 2 and 3 on the measures that begin with a dotted half note.
- The first eight measures can be used as a benediction response. This song would be appropriate any time you are focusing on missions, especially if you are sending a mission team to serve.

(DT)

WORDS: Anon., trans. by Jorge Maldonado
MUSIC: Trad. Cuban, arr. by David L. Bone
Trans. © 1988, arr © 2003 Abingdon Press, admin. by The Copyright Co., Nashville, TN 37212

Composer Natalie Sleeth wrote "Go Now in Peace" as a dismissal song. She was a well-known composer of church music who delighted in writing simple, lovely melodies especially suitable for children.

Talk about where to breathe and place the final consonants. Snap on the fourth beat of measures 3, 4, and 7 to show where to place the consonants and take a breath. Encourage the children not to breathe in the middle of the third phrase: "may the love of God surround you everywhere."

Teach the intervals of the perfect 4th down (C to G, measures 5 and 6) and perfect 5th up (C to G, measures 7 and 8). Write the intervals on a large staff and talk about the placement on the staff. If your singers are familiar with the solfège hand signs and syllables ("do-sol"), use them as you sing these intervals.

Do

Sol

Other Ideas:
- Use as a closing song for Sunday school assemblies, choir rehearsals, and worship services.
- Sing in unison or two-part canon.
- Add Orff patterns when the melody is secure.
- Ask the handbell or tone chime choir to provide accompaniment.
- Add sign language using one of the resources listed on page 6.
- If the children are secure in singing this song, consider asking them to sing this from the aisle of your worship space to encourage the congregation to join in.

(NB)

Go Now in Peace

65

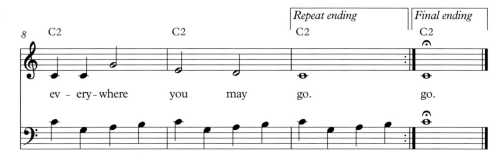

Alto Glockenspiel

Soprano & Alto Metallophones

Alto Xylophone

Bass Xylophone

May be sung as a canon.
Orff instrument patterns may be used alone or in combination on any repetition(s).

WORDS: Natalie Sleeth
MUSIC: Natalie Sleeth
© 1976 Hinshaw Music, Inc. Used with permission.

90

Praising God • Sending Forth

Lord, Make Me More Holy

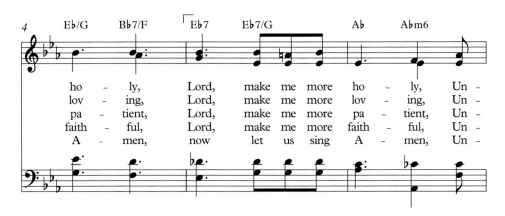

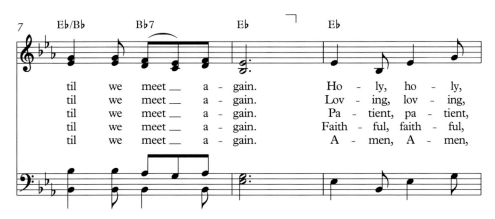

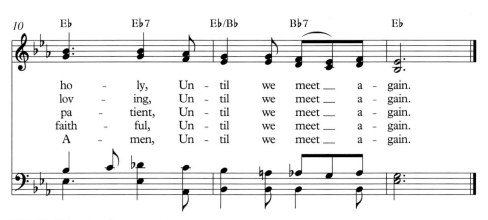

WORDS: African American spiritual
MUSIC: African American spiritual

Praising God • Sending Forth

Using a repetitive text pattern much like "Lord, I Want to Be a Christian," this African American spiritual will become a favorite closing prayer for choir rehearsals, classes, and worship.

Teach this song by rote, lining out each phrase for the children. Help them discover that the melody for the phrase "Until we meet again" is the same and that the first and third phrases are the same except for the last note.

Children can easily learn the sign language for the key words: (HOLY, LOVING, PATIENT, FAITHFUL, AMEN). This will help them learn the key words of the stanzas. Signs can be found on page 8.

Other Ideas:

• Consider creating new stanzas by inserting other words, such as "righteous" or "humble" in place of "holy." One tradition's stanza is "Now, let us say, 'Amen' . . . until we meet again."

• When using this in worship, consider singing the first stanza *a cappella* as the singers sing and sign the text, then add keyboard accompaniment on stanza 2. Gradually increase the dynamics, being careful not to speed up the tempo as the singers move from one dynamic level to the next. You may want to ask the congregation to join the singing of the final stanza.

• Encourage your accompanist to improvise in a gospel style on the accompaniment.

(DT)

The blessing of the prophet Isaiah's words gives us a sense of assurance as we go through our day. Read Isaiah 40:31. Ask the children: "To whom is Isaiah speaking?" "What does it mean "to wait on/for the Lord?" "What is promised to those who wait?"

Write this rhythm on a card.

Define the word *syncopation* and illustrate the concept using this pattern (notes placed off the regular beats). Find this rhythm (or similar pattern) in the song and speak each example. Echo-sing each example.

Echo-speak the text in measure 14, noting that it is different from the previous example. Sing this measure.

Other Ideas:
• Add instruments.

Drums, bongos, or congas:

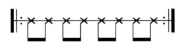

Shaker (maracas, cabasa):

Claves:

• Sing as a benediction for general gatherings, including choir rehearsal, or worship.
• Listen to a recording of ragtime music to explore syncopation. Ragtime is the forerunner of this type of syncopation in contemporary music.

(GW)

May You Run and Not Be Weary

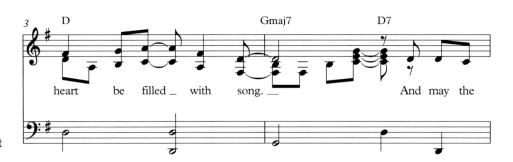

May you run and not __ be wea — ry. __ May your

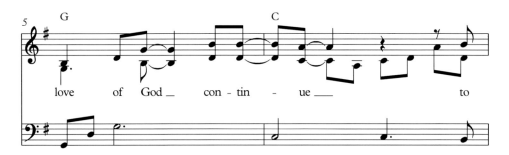

heart be filled __ with song. __ And may the

love of God __ con - tin - ue __ to

give you hope __ and keep you strong. __ And may you

run and not __ be wea — ry. __ May your

WORDS: Paul Murakami and Handt Hanson
MUSIC: Paul Murakami and Handt Hanson
© 1991 Changing Church Forum

Praising God • Sending Forth

life be filled __ with joy! ___ And may the

road you trav - el al - ways lead __ you home. __

May you

Isaiah 55 is a call to the blessings of salvation. Pardon brings peace, happiness, and joy. The earth joins this transformation with shouts of praise as thorns and briars are replaced with trees. God is glorified in our rejoicing. Read Isaiah 55:12-13 and list ways God is glorified.

Accompany this with an autoharp or guitar. Begin with three E minor chords and the children clapping three times (half note pulse), then sing. Add the claps as indicated in the score.

Other Ideas:
- You may use nonpitched percussion instruments on the claps for variety (rhythm sticks, wood block, finger cymbals, triangle).
- Explore the differences in the minor and major tonalities in the first and second sections.
- Sing this in less formal settings, such as Sunday school, vacation Bible school, or summer camp. It may be used as a benediction for worship.
- Create a simple circle dance. Step to the right on the first beat of each measure and close with the left foot on the second beat. Reverse the direction (step left) at measure 17. Each time you dance this dance, lessen the number of measures between switching directions until you are changing directions at the end of each phrase. You may want to have the children hold hands as they dance, dropping them to clap. If you use the extended ending, switch directions every measure as they hold out the word "joy."
- Consider getting faster each time you repeat the song.

(GW)

The Trees of the Field

68

WORDS: Steffi Geiser Ruben (based on Isaiah 55:12)
MUSIC: Stuart Dauermann

Praising God • Sending Forth

Shalom

"Shalom" is a word that has no exact translation in English. It means many different things, such as "farewell," "stay safe," or "have peace." This text is a traditional Hebrew blessing, a blessing to be carried throughout a person's life.

Hebrew Pronunciation Guide:
Shah-LOHM kah-vey-REEM, leh-HEET-rah-OHT

Many children will already know this song, although they may not have learned the same melody or translation. Share with the children that this is a traditional Israeli melody that was handed down through oral tradition. In that same tradition, you will teach the tune that will be used when you sing this song in worship. Teach the melody by rote, phrase by phrase, until the children are comfortable with it.

A simple circle movement game will help the children learn the song. Create two circles, one inside the other. The children should face each other and shake hands to the beat as they sing the first four measures. As they sing "Lehitraot" they drop hands and walk in a circle (one circle moves clockwise, the other counterclockwise) until they sing the words "Shalom" to a new partner. Continue singing and walking several more times.

Other Ideas:
• Try singing in two- or three-part canon.
• Orff instruments, handchimes, or handbells can play the chords as noted on the score on beats 1 and 3 as accompaniment.
• A flute or clarinet player can play one of the canon lines.

(DT)

Orff Instruments

*May be sung as a round.

WORDS: Trad. Hebrew blessing; trans. by Roger N. Deschner
MUSIC: Israeli melody; Orff arr. by Emily R. Brink
Trans. © 1982 The United Methodist Publishing House; Orff arr. © 1994 CRC Publications

Praising God • Sending Forth

Thuma Mina
(Send Me, Lord)

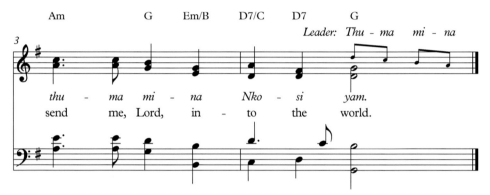

WORDS: Traditional South Africa
MUSIC: Traditional South Africa; transcribed by David Dargle
Transcription © 1983 David Dargle. Administered by Choristers Guild.

This version of this South African song was written as a result of a series of composition workshops held by David Dargle. The text is in Zulu, which most people find to be an easy language to sing.

Use a hand drum to keep the pulse steady as you sing the song to the singers line by line, inviting them to repeat each phrase after you. Ask the singers to join you as you gently sway from side to side as you sing the song.

Zulu Pronunciation Guide:

TOO-mah MEE-nah
NKOH-see yahm.

(The *N* of *Nkosi* is said very quickly, like a hum with your tongue on the roof of your mouth.)

David Dargle taught this handshake to Michael Hawn as a sign of solidarity from the Lesotho (leh-SOO-too) tribe.
1. Shake hands once.
2. Slide hands forward and together to grasp each other's thumbs.
3. Return to the original handshake.
4. Snap your fingers.
Encourage the singers and congregation to use this handshake on the half note pulse as you sing the song.

In South Africa this song is often sung unaccompanied.

Other Ideas:
• Use this as a joyful response to the closing prayer for rehearsals and as the sending forth or as a benediction response for your worship services.
• The phrase that the leader sings at the end leads the children and the congregation into repeating the song. Sing it several times, swaying in time to the music.

(DT)

Two Fishermen

Jesus called his disciples by name to come and follow him. Others, including Susanna, Mary, and Mary Magdalene, traveled with them as Jesus ministered. Jesus continues calling people today to serve and follow him.

Teach the refrain, noting the melodic repetition in the last two measures. For brevity, have soloists or small ensembles sing the stanzas with all responding on the refrain.

Play a dotted quarter pulse on a hand drum as all echo-chant the stanza in rhythm. When they are comfortable chanting the text, have the melody played on a piano as the singers chant. Do they notice that measures 1-8 sound identical to measures 9-16?

Other Ideas:

• Learn more from these scriptures: Matthew 4:18-22; Mark 1:16-20; Luke 5:1-11 and 8:1-3. Ask the singers to list everyone named in this song. Can they find other names in the scriptures verses? Have them add their own names to the list as followers of Jesus.

• Give your thespians a chance to act out this song. You will need children to mime Jesus, James, and John during stanzas 1 and 2. Help them discover how they can use their actions to tell the story the choir is singing. Consider asking different children to call out the names mentioned in the text of stanza 3 as the stanza is sung. On stanza 4, several of the singers could move into the congregation and motion to them, as if calling them today. Add simple choreography to the refrain and dress all the children in biblical costumes. Add a few fishnets and a small boat for a set and you have mini-musical production.

WORDS: Suzanne Toolan (based on Matthew 4:18-22; Mark 1:16-20; Luke 5:1-11; 8:1-3; John 1:40-42)
MUSIC: Suzanne Toolan
© 1970 by GIA Publications, Inc. All rights reserved.

God's Story • Bible Stories

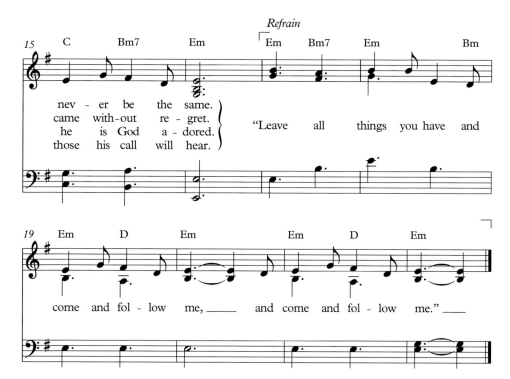

15 C   Bm7   Em   Refrain Em   Bm7   Em   Bm

nev - er be the same.
came with-out re - gret.
he is God a - dored.
those his call will hear.

"Leave all things you have and

19 Em   D   Em   Em   D   Em

come and fol - low me, _____ and come and fol - low me." _____

- Sing this as a general anthem in worship with themes on God's call.
- It may also be used in place of the scripture lesson when this story appears as a reading.
- Sing in Sunday school when learning about God's calling of the disciples and others.

(GW)

Based on Acts 3:1-8, the text tells the story of a man disabled from birth. He spent every day at the gate of the Temple asking for money. When Peter and John stopped to speak with him, his life was drastically changed. Peter and John did not have money to give, but they shared their love for Christ and the healing that comes to us through Christ.

As an introduction, take the time to discuss the word *lame*. That word has taken on a different connotation over the years and children often think of it in a negative way. The lame man had to put his trust in Christ in order to receive the blessing of Christ's healing.

Have the children dramatize the story and take turns playing the part of the lame man, Peter and John, and the crowd of witnesses. Talk with the children about how the people responded when they saw the man walk for the first time. Let their imaginations come alive as they walk and leap for joy.

Set in 6/8, this song has a rocking lilt to it. Ask the children to stand in a circle and step in time (moving clockwise) to the dotted quarter note. Listen as they move and speak. Are they saying the text clearly in unison?

Simple actions for all make this a fun song.
1. Fold hands, as in prayer.
2. Hold out palms.
3. Hold out empty hands, shake head.
4. Extend hands.
5. Point upward.
6. Sweep hands upward.
7. March (in place).
8. Jump up.
9. Raise arms.

(KE)

Silver and Gold Have I None

WORDS: Based on Acts 3:1-8
MUSIC: Anonymous; arr. by Betty Pulkingham
Arr. © 1974 Celebration. All rights reserved. International copyright secured. Used by permission.

God's Story • Bible Stories

15

Christ _____ of Naz - a - reth, rise up and walk."

75 When Jesus Saw the Fishermen

1. When Je - sus saw the fish - er - men in
2. They fol - lowed where he healed the sick and
3. And now his friends are ev - ery - where; the

boats up - on the sea, _____ he called to them, "Come,
gave the hun - gry bread. _____ And oth - ers joined them
cir - cle once so small _____ ex - tends a - round the

leave your nets and fol - low, fol - low me." _____
as they went, wher - ev - er Je - sus led. _____
whole wide world, for Je - sus calls us all. _____

WORDS: Edith Agnew (based on Matthew 4:18-25; Mark 1:16-20; Luke 5:1-11)
MUSIC: Richard L. Van Oss

Words © 1963 W. L. Jenkins. From *Songs and Hymns for Primary Children.* Used by permission of Westminster John Knox Press. Music © 1994 CRC Publications.

- "I Have Decided to Follow Jesus" (page 174) would make a good companion song, as would the popular song, "Lord, You Have Come to the Lakeshore" by Cesareo Gabaraín.
- Use in an assembly or a worship service that deals with the calling of disciples.
- The example on the *FaithSongs* CD adds two measures of accompaniment at the end to give you the option of singing the stanza in a two-part canon.

(NB)

Teach this song with the story of Jesus' call to the disciples. Remind the children that Jesus calls disciples even today. Discuss what it means to "follow Jesus."

Create movement that stresses the duple (two beats per measure) rhythm. Examples might be patsch, clap, patsch, clap; or right snap, left snap, right snap, left snap. Invite the singers to invent movements that express this rhythm and to use them as they sing.

If you are presenting this song to others in worship or another assembly, sing stanza 3 in unison once, then add the canon parts on the repeat(s).

Choose a small group to pantomime as the children sing the song. Stanza 1: Fishermen are fishing; Jesus beckons to them and they follow him. Stanza 2: Jesus heals the sick and the disciples give bread to the hungry; others follow. Stanza 3: Those in the pantomime join hands with the singers and create a circle.

Other Ideas:
- For a folklike feel, sing in unison and play on acoustic guitar. Add a short interlude between the stanzas (for example, the last two measures). You could repeat the last verse in canon, singing it as many times as desired.

Peter acknowledged Jesus as the Christ, the Son of the living God. Jesus identified Peter as the rock on which the church would be built. Read about the naming of Peter in John 1:40-42 and this later encounter with Christ in Matthew 16:13-19.

Write this rhythm on a card.

Treat the dotted eighth and six-teenth pattern as a long-short relationship, similar to swing eighths. Clap or play the pattern on rhythm instruments. Locate examples of the pattern in the song.

Set the quarter note pulse by tapping a hand drum. Speak the text in rhythm. Echo with melody. Children find this to be a fun song to sing and will pick it up easily.

Other Ideas:

- Play the optional voice part rhythm using percussion instruments, such as hand drums or rhythm sticks. Teach the optional melody using scale steps based on D minor.
- Sing at casual gatherings, such as VBS or summer camp.
- Make fists and tap them on top of each other as you sing the Voice 2 part of this song. Divide your group into two smaller groups. As they sing, help the Voice 1 group to work on singing the phrases *legato* as the Voice 2 group "Peter rocks" with the hand motion. Switch back and forth to give each group a chance to sing both parts.

(GW)

Peter Rock

WORDS: James Ritchie; based on John 1:40-42; Matthew 16:13-20
MUSIC: James Ritchie; arr. by David L. Bone

God's Story • Bible Stories

God's Story • Bible Stories

Use this catchy text to memorize the names of the disciples. Read Matthew 10:1-4 to see the list in their scriptural context.

Write each name on the board and guide the children in pronouncing it. Discuss the role of the disciples. Matthew 10 will provide some guidance.

This melody has four phrases. Phrases 1, 2, and 4 are identical. Teach these first, noting their similarity. Teach phrase 3, noting the similarity of the first two measures with the last two measures of the phrase.

This melody is based on a pentatonic scale—a scale made of five pitches containing no half steps. It is easy to improvise an accompaniment using barred Orff instruments. Set up each instrument with only the following notes: D, E, G, A, and B. Remove all other bars.

Establish the tempo by tapping the beat on a hand drum. Invite the children to improvise any pattern as everyone sings. You may include rhythm instruments, such as finger cymbals, claves, wood block, or rhythm sticks, tapping the pulse.

Other Ideas:
- As a pentatonic melody, this can also be sung in canon. Try starting groups six measures apart, one measure apart, and even two beats apart.
- Sing at general gatherings, such as Sunday school, VBS, and church camp.
- May be used in worship as a general song with sermon themes on the calling of the Twelve.

(GW)

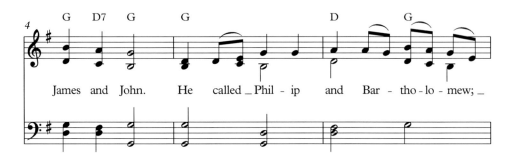

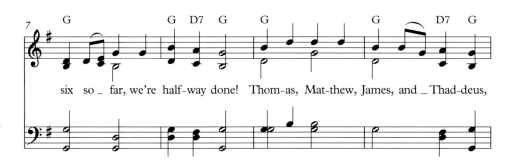

WORDS: Frank DeVries
MUSIC: William Moore
Words © 1982 CRC Publications

God's Story • Bible Stories

Advent Candle Song

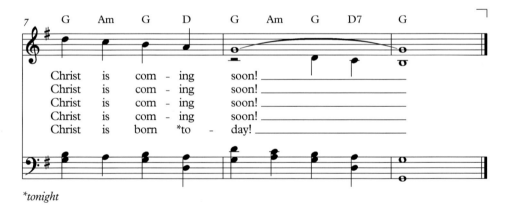

*tonight

Ostinati for Handbells or Orff Instruments

WORDS: Sally Ahner
MUSIC: Sally Ahner; piano acc. arr. by David L. Bone
© 1992, 2003 Abingdon Press, admin. by The Copyright Co., Nashville, TN 37212

God's Story • Advent

This song is ideal for the lighting of the Advent wreath. This song should be sung frequently enough in Advent so that families can sing it at home when they light their own Advent candles each evening.

To help the children place Advent within the church year, use this short poem by Helen Kemp:

Advent, Christmas, Epiphany, Lent
Easter, Ascension, and a Pentecost Event.

© 1995 Cokesbury

Consider creating an Advent wreath using children as the candles. Choose five children to stand tall in the shape of an Advent wreath. With each new stanza, add a flame to a candle by asking the child to raise both hands high above the head, placing palms together. This will create the shape of a candle flame.

Other Ideas:
- Use the handbell and/or Orff parts.
- For an alternate accompaniment, play a descending major scale, beginning on high D and going to low D (one sharp, G major) throughout the song. Handchimes, handbells, flute, or any other instrument could play this pattern.
- Encourage families to extend the ritual of the Advent wreath to their own homes. Use the Advent wreath as a table centerpiece during the evening meal. Lighting the candles each evening will help the children observe the progression of the season to Christmas Eve. Sing the song in a cumulative manner, adding a stanza each week until the entire song is sung on Christmas Eve.

(JH)

Explore the messages of Advent and Palm Sunday. In Advent, talk with the children about what it means for peace and justice to be with us and how hard it is to wait during this season. In preparation for Palm Sunday, discuss the excitement of the crowds that greeted Jesus on the way to Jerusalem. The people believed that their wait for an earthly king was over. Contrast their reaction with discussion about the real reason Jesus entered Jerusalem.

Begin singing this song at a medium tempo, clapping each time on the rest following the word "glory." Sing the song at a fairly slow tempo, getting slightly faster with each repeat.

A circle dance is a fun way to add movement to this song. In a circle:

1. Step to the right with your right foot.
2. Cross your left foot behind and step.
3. Step to the right with your right foot.
4. Cross your left foot in front and step with the left foot.
5. Repeat these four steps for the entire song. Try this starting slow and getting faster!

Other Ideas:

- You may want to consider creating your own text. Have the group work together to create a new text for other Sundays.
- Use as a call to worship or as a response to the scripture. The congregation/choir can perform a line dance by dancing the circle dance steps two times, then reversing the directions (moving to the left). Can they clap and dance?
- Add tambourine, drums, claves, guitar, and bass for instrumental accompaniment.

(DT)

Dance and Sing, for the Lord Will Be with Us

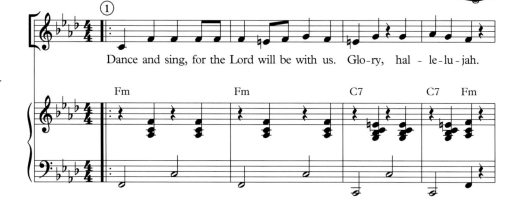

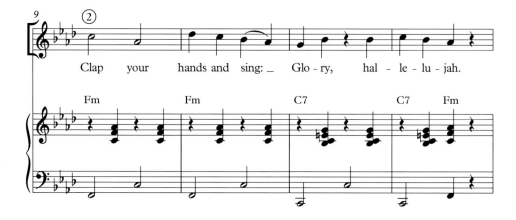

WORDS: Isaiah 11:1-7
MUSIC: Ancient Hebrew folk melody, arr. by Hal H. Hopson
Words © 1998 Choristers Guild

God's Story • Advent

Holy Baby, Holy Child

Discuss the text, "you bring us hope, you bring us peace; you bring us joy, you bring us love." What are hope, peace, joy, and love? How does Jesus bring these gifts to us? What gifts can we offer in return?

Decide on the phrasing you will use before teaching the song (breathing at every point of punctuation or less frequently). Concentrate on maintaining good singing posture and breathing deeply at the beginning of each phrase.

Encourage correct singing of the descending fifth (G to C) in measure 1 to avoid sliding from the upper note to the lower note. Ask the singers to sing measures 1-4, but make each note *staccato* (very short). This prevents sliding between notes. When this is secure, invite them to sing *legato* (smoothly). Listen to be sure that they do not slide between the G and C.

Other Ideas:
- This lovely song is appropriate for use during Advent, as we anticipate the birth of Jesus. It works well at the beginning of a worship service as a call to worship or as a response to a prayer. It could also be used during the lighting of the Advent wreath.
- Let the children introduce the song to the congregation and then lead the congregation in singing it, perhaps for each of the four Sundays in Advent.
- Add motions to visually interpret this text.

(NB)

WORDS: Lynn S. Hurst
MUSIC: Lynn S. Hurst, arr. by Allen Tuten
© 2002 Abingdon Press, admin. by The Copyright Co., Nashville, TN 37212

God's Story • Advent

Advent is a very special time of preparation, a time of getting ready for the birth of the Christ Child. During the four weeks just before Christmas Day, Christians around the world are preparing their hearts to welcome the Baby Jesus who came to bring peace to the entire world.

Echo-chant the text of the refrain in rhythm. Devise a simple "hand-jive" pattern to use while you learn the text. The melody will come easily once the text rhythm is secure.

The stanzas recall familiar verses from Isaiah. Have the children read these four verses and identify them in the song text: Isaiah 9:2; 11:1; 11:6; 40:4.

Other Ideas:
• Use simple percussion patterns on the refrain: hand drum, tambourine, maracas, or shakers.
• Devise a simple choir chime accompaniment for the stanzas. Assign each of the six bells to a ringer.

Bells Used

Assign a shape to each chord. Tell each player which shapes they should play on.

◯ G B D
▢ G C E
▲ A C E
✚ A G D

Hold up large cards with these shapes so that the ringers can ring on the downbeat of each measure. The last measure should only be held for one and a half beats.

Get Ready!

Lively, excited

Refrain

Get read-y! Get read-y! A Sav-ior is com-ing. Get read-y! Get read-y! No time to de-lay. __ Get read-y! Get read-y! A Sav-ior is com-ing. Em-man-u-el is on the way. __

1. A child will soon be born to us __ to
2. A shoot will spring from Jes-se's stem __ and
3. The wolf will live be-side the lamb, __ the
4. The moun-tains all will be made low, __ the

*Upper octave may be omitted.

WORDS: Isaiah 9:2; 11:1, 6; 40:4
MUSIC: Mark Burrows

God's Story • Advent

Measure	Shape
9	❏
10	◯
11	❏
12	◯
13	❏
14	◯
15	▲
16	✚

(KE)

The Advent season is about preparation and waiting—waiting for the Light of the World to come. It is also the beginning of the Christian Year. This anthem has four stanzas, one for each week of Advent. Build the excitement of the season as you teach each stanza. Visit the sanctuary to see, touch, and discuss the Advent wreath.

Create a rhythm chart for the melody. Assign these note lengths to specific body percussions:

Eighth notes = alternating snaps or patschen (patting the thighs)
Quarter notes = claps
Whole note = slide palms slowly down to knees

Tap a half note pulse on a hand drum as the children do the body percussions for the rhythms.

Challenge the children to find the two phrases that share the same rhythm (phrases 1 and 2). Speak the text in rhythm.

This melody is based on a D major scale. Write on the board a scale pattern using numbers or solfège. Teach the melody by pointing to the corresponding pitch number/syllable.

Other Ideas:
• Add instruments:

Handbells or alto metallophone:

Finger cymbals:

• Sing each week in Advent as a call or response to the lighting of the Advent wreath. Sing stanza 1 on week 1. Sing stanzas 1 and 2 on week 2. Continue until all stanzas are sung on week 4.

(GW)

Light One Candle for Waiting

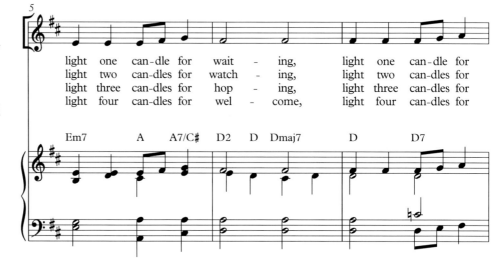

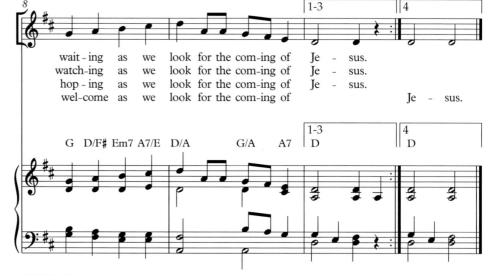

WORDS: Michael Bedford
MUSIC: Michael Bedford
© 2000 Choristers Guild

God's Story • Advent

like a child

1. like a child love would send to re-veal and to mend, like a
2. like a child we will meet, rag-ged clothes dirt-y feet like a
3. like a child born to pray and to show us the way, like a

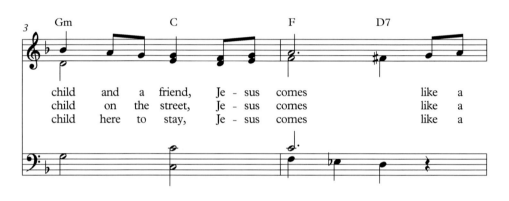

child and a friend, Je-sus comes like a
child on the street, Je-sus comes like a
child here to stay, Je-sus comes like a

child we may find claim-ing heart soul and mind, like a
child we once knew com-ing back in-to view, like a
child we re-ceive all that love can con-ceive, like a

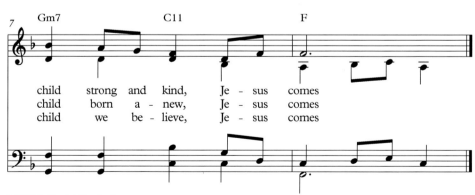

child strong and kind, Je-sus comes
child born a-new, Je-sus comes
child we be-lieve, Je-sus comes

WORDS: Daniel Charles Damon
MUSIC: Daniel Charles Damon

Many traditional images used for Jesus are foreign to contemporary children (master, shepherd, and so on). Dan Damon wrote this hymn for a children's camp, using images for Jesus that he felt children could understand. The composer's use of lowercase letters is intentional. Only the name of Jesus includes an uppercase letter. Use this as a discussion starter with the children about the importance of Jesus in their lives.

This hymn is sometimes associated with the Gospel accounts of Jesus welcoming the children and rebuking the disciples for denying their access to him. This hymn text suggests that the kingdom of God sometimes comes to us in the guise of a child, and that all should accept and welcome children as signs of God's presence.

Use the melodic fragment that carries "like a child" to help learn this song. It happens four times each stanza and always on the same three pitches. This tiny motif is the key to learning the song.

Mark a piano or keyboard with removable sticky dots to help the children locate all the occurrences of G-A-B♭ and then assign children to those positions. They will enjoy playing along when the motif occurs in the melody. This will reinforce the tune.

Other Ideas:
- Assist the children in developing a pantomime or short dramatic skit to the story of "Jesus and the Children" (Matthew 19:13-15; Mark 10:13-16; Luke 18:15-17). Use it to lead into singing the song.
- It may be used in Advent, Christmas, and Epiphany seasons or when this Gospel lesson appears in the lectionary. It is also very appropriate for Children's Sabbath, which occurs in October each year.

(JH)

Prepare the Royal Highway

The prophet Isaiah foretold the coming of Christ. He told the people to get ready. Advent is celebrated on the four Sundays prior to Christmas when the church prepares for the birth of Christ and for the second coming of the Messiah. How does your church celebrate Advent? Do you light candles each week and decorate the sanctuary? Is there a special chrismon tree?

Read Isaiah 40 (especially verses 3-5) to hear the words of the prophet. What stanza of this song is based on the Isaiah passage?

Echo-chant the text in two-measure phrases. Help the singers feel the lilting quality of the meter. Use a tempo that keeps the text easy to declaim but that has movement and joy.

Other Ideas:
• Add instruments.
  Hand drum, tambourine, wood block: First and last beat of each measure.
  Finger cymbals, claves, jingles: First beat of each measure.
• Sing as a hymn or general anthem during Advent or as a processional on Palm/Passion Sunday.
• Sing one stanza each week in Advent in conjunction with the lighting of the Advent wreath. Consider teaching the refrain to the congregation so they can join in each week.
• Make this a multigenerational anthem combining all age groups. Have the youngest choir sing only the refrain, teaching it to the congregation. Each choir sings a stanza, with all joining on the refrain.
• If you are using the *FaithSongs* CD, there is one measure of G inserted between each stanza to give your singers a chance to get a good breath between stanzas.

(GW)

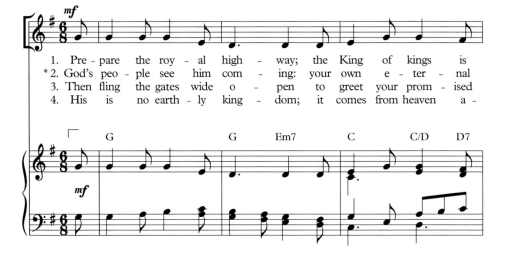

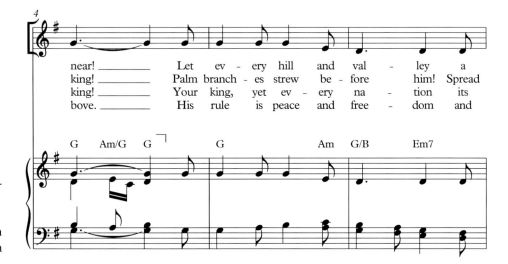

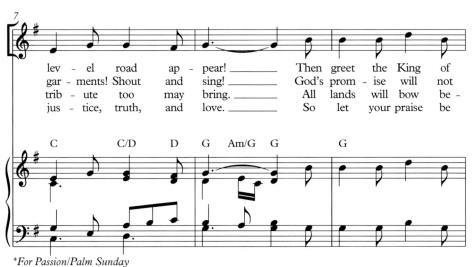

*For Passion/Palm Sunday

WORDS: Frans Mikael Franzén; trans. *Lutheran Book of Worship*
MUSIC: Swedish traditional; arr. by John D. Horman
Trans. © 1978 Lutheran Book of Worship; arr. © 2003 Abingdon Press, admin. by The Copyright Co., Nashville, TN 37212

glo - ry, fore - told in sa - cred sto - ry:
fail you! No more shall doubt __ as - sail __ you! } Ho -
fore him; their voic - es join __ your sing - ing:
sound - ing for kind - ness so __ a - bound - ing:

D   D   C   C/D

poco rit.   *a tempo*

san - na to __ the __ Lord, __ for he ful - fills __ God's Word! __

G   C/E   Bm7   Cmaj7   C/D   D7   G

poco rit.   *a tempo*

The text of "Magnificat" is based on a song attributed to Mary, who was expecting the birth of her baby, Jesus. The song is often called "Mary's Song." "Magnificat" is a Latin word that pertains to greatness. Mary praises God for doing "great things" for her and Abraham's descendants. Many composers have written musical settings of this text (for example, Palestrina, J. S. Bach, and John Rutter).

Explain that the word *magnify* means to "praise highly" or "to glorify."

Latin Pronunciation Guide:
mahn-NYEE-fee-caht
AH-knee-mah MEH-ah
DOH-mee-noom
(The "ng" in the word *magnificat* is like the "gn" in *lasagna*.)

Before singing in canon, use an instrument to play the second canon part. Sing in a two-part canon, moving to a three-part, then four-part canon.

Other Ideas:
• Especially appropriate during Advent when the "Song of Mary" is one of the suggested lectionary scriptures for the day, either the third or fourth Sunday of Advent.
• Develop a reading using the song as a sung response.
   Sing the song once in unison.
   Read Luke 1:46-49.
   Sing the song once in unison.
   Read Luke 1:50-53.
   Sing the song once in unison or canon.
   Read Luke 1:54-55.
   Sing the song once in unison or canon, adding the descant.
• The voices on the *FaithSongs* CD sing the first canon, then the second canon, and then sing them together. By turning down the voices you can sing either canon as a two-part canon.

(NB)

Magnificat

WORDS: Luke 1:46
MUSIC: Jacques Berthier

© 1978 Les Presses de Taizé (France). Used by permission of GIA Publications, Inc., exclusive agent. All rights reserved.

God's Story • Advent

Children, Go Where I Send You

Alternate text:
1. ... one by one; one for the little bitty baby ...
2. ... two by two; two for Paul and Silas, ...
3. ... three by three; three for the Hebrew children, ...
4. ... four by four; four for the four come a-knockin' at the door, ...
5. ... five by five; five for the gospel preachers, ...
6. ... six by six; six for the six that never got fixed, ...

* Stanzas are cumulative; each time a new stanza is sung, the previous stanzas are repeated from the asterisk.

WORDS: African American spiritual
MUSIC: African American spiritual; arr. by John D. Horman
Arr. © 2003 Abingdon Press, admin. by The Copyright Co., Nashville, TN 37212

God's Story • Christmas and Epiphany

The Nativity sparks the child's imagination as one wonders what it was like that special night in Bethlehem. Read Luke 2:1-20 as an introduction to discussing this blessed event with the children. If you are teaching the alternate text, also discuss the stories of those characters.

This spiritual began as a teaching song for children who were not allowed to go to school. They could learn both their "numbers" and Bible stories.

Create a mural based on the stanzas. Include six stars, five snowflakes, four oxen, and so forth, based on the text you are teaching. Display the completed picture in the rehearsal room and use as a guide to learning the stanzas.

Begin with a leader singing the first six measures. The singers enter at measure 6, each time counting backward, repeating measures 7-8. Assign stanzas to individual or groups of children who stand and sing when their number is sung.

Other Ideas:
• Add instruments:

Bass / Alto Xylophone:

Glockenspiel:

Bongos:

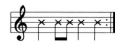

Shaker:

• Sing in teaching gatherings with children, such as Sunday school, VBS, or church camp.
• The Christmas text may be used in response to Nativity scripture in worship.

(GW)

117

This is a Hispanic folk hymn from New Mexico. "A la ru, a la mé" is a sequence of nonsense syllables with no apparent meaning except for the soothing effect of their warm vowel sounds.

Ask the children what kind of song this is: (a) march; (b) lullaby; (c) dance; or (d) walking song.

Who is singing the song? (Mary to the baby Jesus.) Why does Mary have "pangs of sorrow?" (Perhaps because of Jesus' humble birth, or because she foresees the suffering he will endure in his life.)

Add percussion to this song: Drum, maracas, claves, and finger cymbals. Avoid louder instruments. This is a lullaby and we don't want to "wake" the baby.

Other Ideas:
- Add the descant for bells or Orff-style barred instruments on the refrain.
- Discuss with the children what happened in the story of Jesus' Nativity after the birth in Bethlehem (Matthew 2):
  - ❏ Arrival of the Kings
  - ❏ Slaughter of the Innocents
  - ❏ The Flight into Egypt
- Ask someone in your community who speaks Spanish fluently to come and help your children with the pronunciation if needed.

(JH)

Bell Obbligato:

Duérmete, Niño Lindo
(Oh, Sleep Now, Holy Baby)

89

1. Duér-me-te ni-ño lin-do, _____ en los bra-zos del _____ a-mor _____ mien-tras que duer-me y des-can-sa _____ la pe-na de mi do-lor. A-la ru, _____ a-la mé, _____ a-la ru, _____ a la mé, _____ a la ru, a la ru, a la mé. _____

1. Oh, sleep _ now, ho-ly ba-by, _____ with your head a-gainst _ my breast; _____ mean-while the pangs of my sor-row _____ are soothed and put _ to rest.

2. No temas al rey Herodes
que nada te ha de hacer;
en los brazos de tu madre
y ahi nadie te ha de ofender.

2. You need not fear King Herod,
he will bring no harm to you;
so rest in the arms of your mother
who sings you a la ru.

WORDS: Hispanic folk song, trans. by John Donald Robb
MUSIC: Hispanic folk tune, arr. by John Donald Robb
Trans. and arr. © 1954 University of New Mexico Foundation, Robb Musical Trust

Go, Tell It on the Mountain

90 *Refrain*

Go, tell it on the moun-tain, o-ver the hills and ev-ery-where, Go, tell it on the moun-tain that Je-sus Christ __ is born.

Fine

1. While shep-herds kept their
2. The shep-herds feared and
3. Down in a low-ly

watch-ing o'er si-lent flocks by night, Be-
trem-bled when lo! a-bove the earth rang
man-ger the hum-ble Christ was born, and

hold through-out the heav-ens there shone a ho-ly light. ____
out the an-gel cho-rus that hailed our Sav-ior's birth. ____
God sent us sal-va-tion that bless-ed Christ-mas morn. ____

D.C.

WORDS: African American spiritual, adapt. by John W. Work, Jr.
MUSIC: African American spiritual, arr. by John W. Work, Jr.
Adapt. © 1940 John W. Work, Jr.; harm. © 1965 Abingdon Press, admin. by The Copyright Co., Nashville, TN 37212

God's Story • Christmas and Epiphany

The refrain of "Go, Tell It on the Mountain" is an African American spiritual that has been passed down from person to person for many years. John Wesley Work, Jr. (1872–1925) and his brother, Frederick Jerome, were prominent figures in the preservation of spirituals. They published several collections of slave songs and spirituals.

Begin by teaching only the "Go, tell it on the mountain" part of the melody. How many times does it occur in the refrain? (Two.) What questions are answered by the text? (Where and why.)

Listen next to the text of the stanzas and discuss what questions are answered (when, what, who, and where).

Other Ideas:
• Add an Orff-style accompaniment to the refrain.
• Providing an opportunity to create original stanzas to this spiritual can be rewarding for both teacher and children. It also recreates the kind of spontaneous creation of text that characterized the genesis of many spirituals. Point out the importance of counting syllables and adhering to that count. Be sure that accents fall with important words and that syllables fall on strong beats within the melody. The syllabic count: 7 6 7 6.

(JH)

Go, Tell It on the Mountain (refrain)

Xylophones

Glockenspiels

Long, Long Ago

This is a vivid depiction of the night Jesus was born. Read about Jesus' birth in Luke 2:1-20.

The gentle, *legato* nature of this melody may be expressed by singing quietly on "loo" as if singing a lullaby. Notice that the rhythm pattern in measures 3-6 is repeated in measures 7-10. Similar patterns are used in stanza 3 and the coda. Can your singers find them?

Dynamics are important in communicating the story. Sing stanzas 1, 2, and 4 quietly, as if you would not wake the baby Jesus. Stanza 3 is stronger, when the angels sing "their songs of joy."

Other Ideas:
- Add a guitar to the accompaniment.
- Sing as an anthem for worship in Christmastide or in a Lessons and Carols service following the appropriate scripture.
- Use inexpensive capiz shell wind chimes played softly during the introduction to help the children "hear" the gentle rattle of the olive leaves moving. Play inexpensive tinkling bell-sounding wind chimes softly on stanza 3 to announce the angels.

(GW)

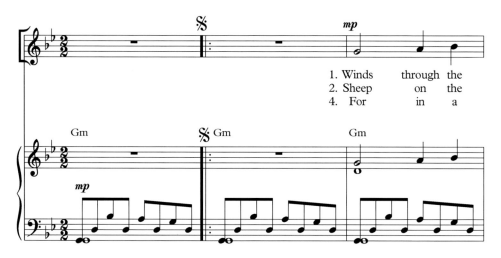

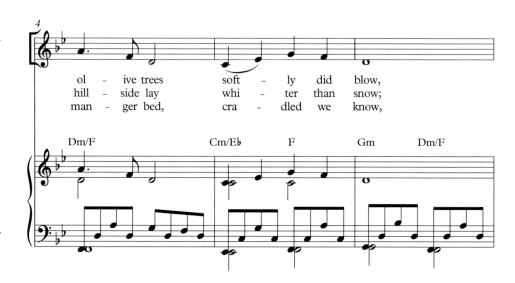

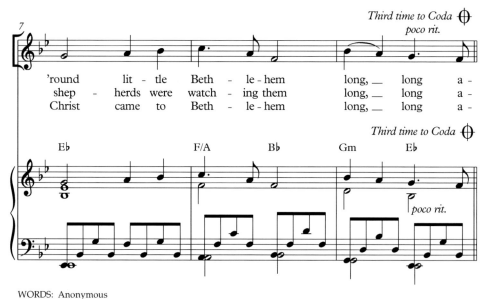

Anthem Setting: "Long Long Ago" by Gary Alan Smith (Abingdon Press 501717). Unison treble voices (optional two-part) and piano with optional guitar.

WORDS: Anonymous
MUSIC: Gary Alan Smith
© 1980, 1995 Gamut Music Productions

go.   Christ came to Beth - le-hem long, ____

long   a - go.

One Holy Night in Bethlehem

1. One holy night in Bethlehem the
2. Their music echoed through the town in
3. As Joseph touched the lamb's soft wool and
4. Be still and you will hear tonight these

air was filled with song. Angelic voices
to the stable stall, where Mary sang a
fed the donkey hay, he whistled his own
melodies of old. Then join your voice in

sang on high and shepherds piped along: *Refrain*
lullaby and rocked her baby small: Sing
happy tune and thanked God for this day:
harmony until the tale is told:

glory, glory, gloria! God's love is given birth! Be

not afraid! Sing gloria, and peace to all the earth!

WORDS: Mary Nelson Keithahn
MUSIC: John D. Horman
© 1998 Abingdon Press, admin. by The Copyright Co., Nashville, TN 37212

In this song, we sing of the angels who called out "Gloria" as they announced the birth of Jesus. Look for other scenes in the text as you sing of Mary rocking Jesus, with Joseph and the animals watching.

The stanza begins with two similar phrases. Echo-sing measures 1-4 in two short phrases. Continue the process, singing measures 5-8. Note the first half in each group uses the same melody. Compare the second half in each group.

Ask singers to locate the groups of four eighth notes in this melody. Sing each group, drawing the melodic contour with your hand. Ask, "Are any the same?" "Are any different?" For fun, sing stanza 1 sitting, but stand each time the four eighth note passage appears.

Other Ideas:
- Read about the shepherds and angels in Luke 2:8-20.
- Create tableaus for each stanza. Have a few children step forward as the angels and shepherds for stanza 1. On stanza 2, one child portrays Mary rocking a child, kneeling front center. Joseph walks about the area in stanza 3, as if tending the animals. He joins Mary by the close of this stanza. Bring the entire choir into the tableau for stanza 4.
- Sing this as a prelude or prologue to a Las Posadas service. It may serve as a general anthem during Christmastide.
- Use the refrain as a response to the reading of the Gospel.

(GW)

Anthem Setting: "One Holy Night in Bethlehem" by John D. Horman (Abingdon Press 0687094984). Unison treble choir, unison mixed choir (optional descant), SATB choir, and keyboard.

This exciting carol from the West Indies is a favorite of children all over the world.

Explain the meaning of "He come from the glory, he come from the glorious kingdom." John 1:1-2, 14, 18 reveals that the Word (Jesus) was with God from the beginning of time. In order to fulfill God's plan of grace, Jesus came to earth as a baby, leaving behind his home in glory.

Use the song to create a mini-pageant as the group sings. Select children to be Mary and Joseph, as well as several to be shepherds, angels, and wise men. Mary moves into place on stanza 1. The angels move into place at measure 9, the shepherds move to their places at measure 17. Joseph moves into place during the second stanza with the wise men completing the tableau during the final refrain.

Other Ideas:
• For an intergenerational approach, have the children sing the verses and the youth or adult choir join on the refrain.
• Add percussion instruments (shakers, claves, maracas, bongos).
• To add instrumental interest, consider using a steel drum, xylophone, or marimba patch on a MIDI keyboard.
• The people from the West Indies typically do not stand still when making music. Encourage the children to sway gently, clap lightly, or do simple movements during the song.
• Appropriate for use in worship in late Advent, Christmas Eve/Day, and during Christmastide.

(NB)

Selected and adapted from the musical *The World Sings Noel* by Hal H. Hopson (Abingdon Press, 2000). Unison, two-part, and/or SAB voices and keyboard.

The Virgin Mary Had a Baby Boy

WORDS: Traditional West Indian carol
MUSIC: Traditional West Indian carol; arr. by Hal H. Hopson
Arr. © 2000 Abingdon Press, admin. by The Copyright Co., Nashville, TN 37212

God's Story • Christmas and Epiphany

This text is equally appropriate for Epiphany or themes of stewardship. For an Epiphany study, read the story found in Matthew 2:1-12. You may want to tell the story of "The Gift of the Magi" by O. Henry. During stewardship themes, include the children in your stewardship campaign. Discuss what gifts of time and talent they can and do offer your church. Use stanza 2 to identify gifts children can bring as their offering to God. Add to the list.

Phrases 1, 2, and 4 are similar. Clap the rhythm in these phrases. Note the dotted rhythm in measure 15.

Echo-sing measures 1-2. Discover each occurrence of this melody (measures 1-2, 5-6, 13-14). The first half phrase resembles a call and the second half the response. Have the children sing each call and you sing the response.

Phrase 3 is unique. Echo-sing as two subphrases on "lah," illustrating the melodic contour. Help the children sing the ascending passage with correct vocal posture, careful that the chin does not rise on "the King." As they sing measures 11-12, have them touch the chin and slightly move the head forward and down. This should produce a beautiful head tone.

Other Ideas:
• Explore steady beat. Have the group sit in a circle. Tap the half note pulse with a hand drum to establish and maintain the beat. Take a wicker basket, such as an offering basket or other object, and have the children pass it around the circle on the beat.
• Sing as an anthem for a stewardship theme or in response to the congregation collecting stewardship pledges.
• It may be used during Epiphany with the visit of the Magi.

(GW)

The Wise May Bring Their Learning

WORDS: Anonymous
MUSIC: John D. Horman
Music © 1998 Abingdon Press, admin. by The Copyright Co., Nashville, TN 37212

God's Story • Christmas and Epiphany

O How He Loves You and Me

95

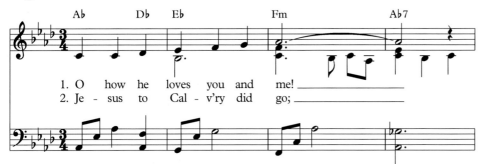

1. O how he loves you and me! _____
2. Je - sus to Cal - v'ry did go; _____

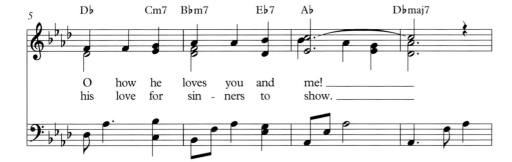

O how he loves you and me! _____
his love for sin - ners to show. _____

He gave his life. What ___ more could he give?
What he did there brought ___ hope from de - spair.

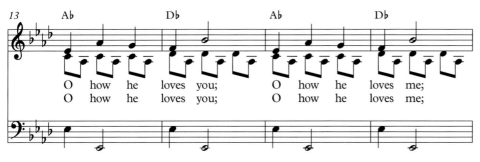

O how he loves you; O how he loves me;
O how he loves you; O how he loves me;

O how he loves you and me! _____
O how he loves you and me! _____

WORDS: Kurt Kaiser
MUSIC: Kurt Kaiser
© 1985 Word Music, Inc.

God's Story • Lent

Talk about Jesus' love for us and his willingness to show that love through his death on the cross. Explain that Calvary (also called "Golgotha") was the hill not far from the walls of Jerusalem where Jesus and those accused of crimes were cruci-fied. Review John 3:16. Ask the children how Jesus' sacrifice "brought hope from despair."

Consider creating an anthem for worship. The song can be sung in a variety of ways:

1. The entire group sings both stanzas.
2. A soloist sings stanza 1, and the group sings stanza 2.
3. Divide the singers into two groups.
   Stanza 1: Group 1 sings meas-ures 1-4; group 2 sings meas-ures 5-8; both groups sing measure 9-12; group 1 sings measures 13-14; group 2 sings measures 15-16; and both groups sing measures 17-20.
   Stanza 2: Both groups sing measures 1-12; group 1 sings measures 13-14; group 2 sings measures 15-16; and both groups sing measures 17-20.
4. Add an instrumental inter-lude between stanzas 1 and 2 (example: measures 9-12 and 17-20).

Other Ideas:

• Reinforce the concept of thinking intervals "higher" as the line ascends. Sing the melody on a neutral syllable, such as "mah," and have the singers "paint a vertical line in the air" as the musical line ascends.
• Use during Lent and Holy Week, or at other times when Christ's sacrifice is the theme. Use in conjunction with the teaching of the Passion narra-tives (Matt. 26–27; Mark 14–15; Luke 22–23; John 18–19).

(NB)

127

The exuberance of Palm /Passion Sunday guides the hymn writer's account of Jesus' entry into Jerusalem. Read about this in Matthew 21:8-9, Mark 11:8-10, Luke 19:36-38, and John 12:12-13. The two stanzas and refrain were composed for the choir of The United Methodist Church in Covington, Virginia, where the author and his two sons were once members. Can you imagine Jesus riding into Jerusalem as you sing the refrain?

Use the last eight measures ("Hosanna") to explore whole, dotted half, half, quarter, and eighth notes. Write the rhythm of these eight measures on a chalkboard or large poster. Clap and count the rhythm. Play the pattern using nonpitched percussion instruments, such as rhythm sticks, wood blocks, or claves. Sing this section, creating your own accompaniment rhythm.

Other Ideas:
• Consider teaching measures 17-24 the refrain to your singers and the congregation in Spanish. This is easily learned and adding the congregation helps build the excitement. The example on the *FaithSong* CD is sung this way.

Spanish Pronunciation Guide:
Oh-SAH-na, Oh-SAH-nahl-Reh!

• This hymn works well as a processional anthem on Palm/Passion Sunday:

1. Stanza (sung by a soloist or small ensemble): Choir walks down the aisle; arrive at least midway to the chancel by the refrain.
2. Refrain movement: Raise right hand (measure 1); raise left hand (measure 2); clasp hands together above the head (measure 3); release hands slowly outward and down creating a circle (measure 4).

128

Mantos y Palmas
(Filled with Excitement)

96

WORDS: Rubén Ruiz Avila; trans. by Gertrude C. Suppe
MUSIC: Rubén Ruiz Avila; arr. by Alvin Schutmaat

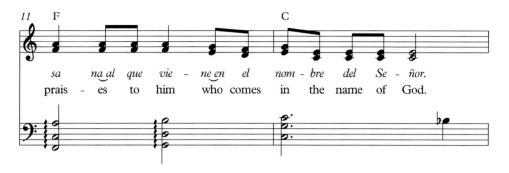

sa na al que vie - ne en el nom - bre del Se - ñor.
prais - es to him who comes in the name of God.

3. Repeat the same movement for the next four measures. Sign the "Hosanna" section.
4. Repeat the process for stanza 2, arriving in the chancel for the final refrain.
5. Repeat the refrain, if needed, to get in place.

• Add sign language: HOSANNA ("HALLELUJAH"), KING

(GW)

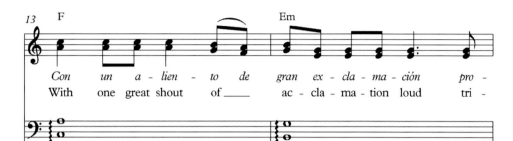

Con un a - lien - to de gran ex - cla - ma - ción pro -
With one great shout of ___ ac - cla - ma - tion loud tri -

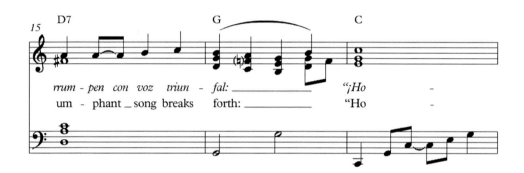

rrum - pen con voz triun - fal: _____ "¡Ho -
um - phant _ song breaks forth: _____ "Ho -

Hosanna

san - na! ¡Ho - san - na al Rey! _
san - na, ho - san - na to the King!

King

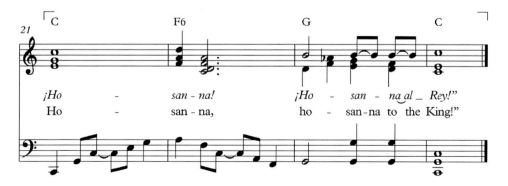

¡Ho - san - na! ¡Ho - san - na al _ Rey!"
Ho - san - na, ho - san - na to the King!"

John Horman dedicated this song to a teacher named Martha Jaquette, who encouraged him and assisted him when he was just beginning to write music. Though he never had any classes with this teacher, she knew of his music and had faith in his ability to write for children. She died in 1999.

Begin by saying the word "Hosanna!" in three different ways:

1. Ho-san-na!

TAH-TAH-TAH

2. Ho—san-na!

TOH—TAH-TAH

3. Ho-san-na!

TAHEE-TAHEE-TAH

After listening to the recording of this song, can the children pick which rhythm is used in the refrain? (The third.)

It is fun to move in two contrasting ways to this song, *marcato* and *legato*. Explain the meaning of these two words: *Marcato* is "punched music." *Legato* is "smooth music."

Instruct the children to move in stark, sudden movements (arms and legs jutting outward at odd angles) to the refrain. This will create energy for the "Hosanna" section. Ask them to move in long, flowing movements (slowly and fluidly) for the stanzas. This will result in wonderful contrast.

Select four to six children, divide them into two groups, and assign either the refrain or stanza sections to each. Instruct the group not moving to "freeze" in place while the other group interprets the

Hosanna in the Highest

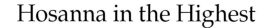

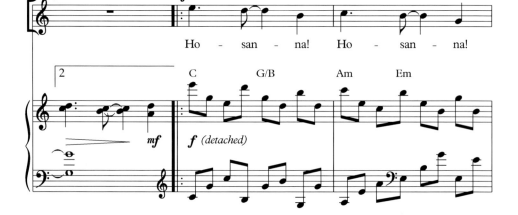

WORDS: John D. Horman
MUSIC: John D. Horman
© 1980, 1999 Abingdon Press, admin. by The Copyright Co., Nashville, TN 37212

God's Story • Lent

music. The remainder of the group sings the song.

Other Ideas:
• Add handbells to the refrain.
• Read Matthew 21:1-11 to discuss the story behind this song.

(JH)

Handbells/Handchimes

God's Story • Lent

Dear Joseph of Arimathea

99

1. Did you know, dear Jo-seph, did you know? _____ Did you
2. Did you cry, dear Jo-seph, did you cry? _____ Did you
3. Had you faith, dear Jo-seph, had you faith? _____ Had you
4. Had you trust, dear Jo-seph, had you trust? _____ Had you

know, dear Jo-seph, did you know? _____ When you
cry, dear Jo-seph, did you cry? _____ When you
faith, dear Jo-seph, had you faith? _____ When you
trust, dear Jo-seph, had you trust? _____ When you

went to Pon-tius Pi-late and you asked for Je-sus'
stood be-neath him, life-less on the cross, his bod-y
wrapped him up in lin-ens and you placed him in the
heard that he had ris-en and was seen a-mong the

bod-y, did you know? _____
hang-ing, did you cry? _____
grave, then had you faith? _____
liv-ing, had you trust? _____

WORDS: Neil MacNaughton, alt.
MUSIC: Neil MacNaughton, arr. by John D. Horman
© 1991 Neil MacNaughton

Tell the children who Joseph of Arimathea was and what role he played in the Crucifixion story (Matt. 27:57-60; Mark 15:43-46; Luke 23:50-53; John 19:38-42). Ask them what feelings Joseph might have experienced when Jesus died. Use the text of the song to help generate ideas.

Connect the song to one of the Gospel accounts of Joseph of Arimathea. Have someone read the scripture as the children hum or "oo" the melody. When the reading is completed, sing the song.

Teach the concept of *legato* (smoothly moving from one note to another, without space between the notes). Have the children sing the melody on a rounded "loo" or other neutral syllable. Encourage them to think of moving from one note to the next as if they were connecting the dots in a puzzle without lifting their pencil from the paper. As they sing each musical phrase, they should use their hands to "connect the notes" (draw a slight arch in the air, moving from left to right).

Other Ideas:

• To help the children hear the haunting quality of the melody, play it on a wind or string instrument (such as flute, recorder, clarinet, oboe, violin, viola, or cello). Adjust the octave as necessary.

• This song works well accompanied by an acoustic guitar. Consider adding one of the instruments listed above, reinforcing the melody or playing a descant.

• Use this late in Lent or during Holy Week. Consider singing stanzas 1-3 for Good Friday worship. Stanza 1 could be sung during an Easter Vigil service or as a part of the beginning of an Easter Sunrise service.

(NB)

God's Story • Lent

We Sang Our Glad Hosannas

The events of Holy Week unfold with each stanza of this hymn. Notice that the author begins with "we," placing the singer in context with the action. How do "we" participate in these events today?

Divide the text of stanza 1 into four-measure phrases and write each section on a large card. After listening to stanza 1 several times, ask a singer to place the cards in the correct order. Ask, "Which of the four phrases have similar melodies?" (The first, second, and fourth.) "How are they similar?" (The first half of each has the same melody.) "Which section is different?" (The third.) "Are two exactly alike?" (The second and fourth.)

Other Ideas:
- Explore the differences between major and minor tonalities.
- Read and discuss the related scripture listed at the bottom of the hymn. Have singers assign specific scripture verses to the stanzas of the hymn text.
- Ask your singers to name the events described in the text. Can they match the events with the day in Holy Week?
- Sing this as a hymn during Holy Week services; as a choir anthem on Palm/ Passion Sunday; stanza 3 for Maundy Thursday; stanza 4 for Good/Holy Friday; stanzas 4 and 5 for Easter Vigil.

(GW)

Anthem Setting: "We Sang Our Glad Hosannas" by John D. Horman (Abingdon Press, 024099). Palm Sunday or Holy Week anthem for combined children's and SATB choirs with keyboard accompaniment.

WORDS: Mary Nelson Keithahn (Matt. 2:1-17; 27:27-31, 55-56; Mark 11:15-19; 14:17-21, 43-50; John 19:38-42; 20:1-18)
MUSIC: John D. Horman
© 1998 Abingdon Press, admin. by The Copyright Co., Nashville, TN 37212

God's Story • Lent

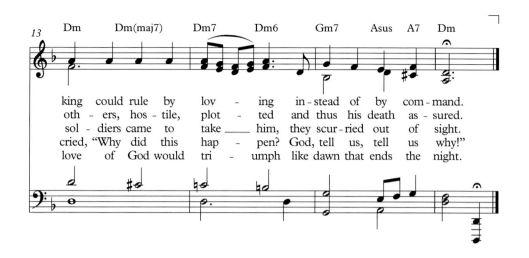

king could rule by lov - ing in-stead of by com-mand.
oth - ers, hos - tile, plot - ted and thus his death as - sured.
sol - diers came to take ___ him, they scur-ried out of sight.
cried, "Why did this hap - pen? God, tell us, tell us why!"
love of God would tri - umph like dawn that ends the night.

He's Alive!

Imagine the pain of witnessing the Crucifixion and then thinking that Jesus' body had be stolen. But the word of joy comes: "He's alive!"

Reinforce the beat of the song by marching in a circle, taking one step on each beat. Use the first two phrases of the song to teach "sequence" (a musical pattern that is repeated at another pitch). The first phrase ("The Lord is risen from the dead") begins on G, the first or tonic note in the key of G major. The second phrase ("The Lord is risen as he said") repeats the musical pattern of the first phrase, but it begins on B, the third note in the G major scale.

Use the third phrase ("He's alive! He's alive!") to teach the interval of an octave. Sing in three-part canon, or use one or more instruments (such as flute, recorder, or piano) to play the parts while the children sing.

Other Ideas:
- Add a finger cymbal or triangle to strike on the word "risen" and on the second syllable of "a-*live*."
- This song would work well as a call to worship, a response to a Scripture reading, or a response to prayer on Easter Sunday.
- If the children feel comfortable with the song, consider using it as a processional during Easter Sunday worship. The children could sing in unison as they walk and begin the canon once they are in the choir loft or other position.

(NB)

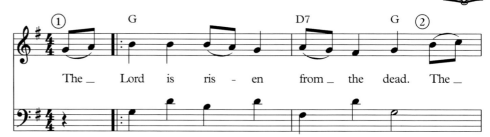

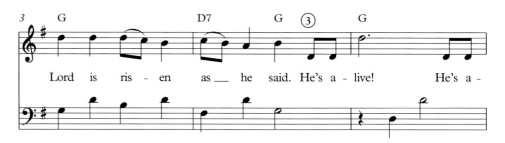

Orff Instruments

WORDS: Tom Fettke
MUSIC: Tom Fettke, arr. by Richard L. Van Oss

God's Story • Easter and Eastertide

Living Christ, Bring Us Love

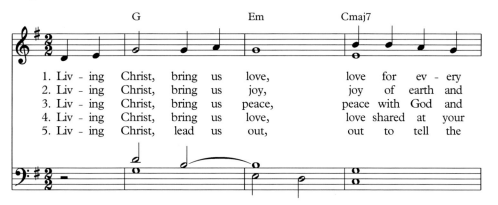

1. Liv - ing Christ, bring us love, love for ev - ery
2. Liv - ing Christ, bring us joy, joy of earth and
3. Liv - ing Christ, bring us peace, peace with God and
4. Liv - ing Christ, bring us love, love shared at your
5. Liv - ing Christ, lead us out, out to tell the

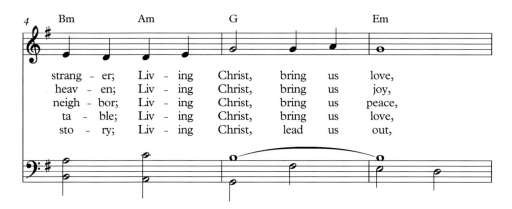

strang - er; Liv - ing Christ, bring us love,
heav - en; Liv - ing Christ, bring us joy,
neigh - bor; Liv - ing Christ, bring us peace,
ta - ble; Liv - ing Christ, bring us love,
sto - ry; Liv - ing Christ, lead us out,

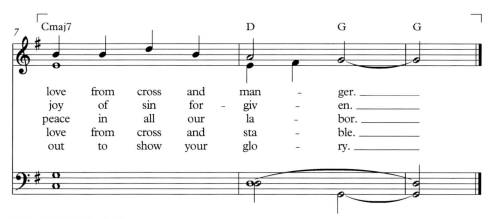

love from cross and man - ger. _____
joy of sin for - giv - en. _____
peace in all our la - bor. _____
love from cross and sta - ble. _____
out to show your glo - ry. _____

WORDS: Daniel Charles Damon
MUSIC: Daniel Charles Damon

This hymn has a "Life of Christ" text, spanning birth to resurrection and beyond.

The children will easily pick up the "Living Christ, bring us love" melody (measures 1-2 and 5-6). Ask them to sing it whenever it happens and, bit by bit, add the missing parts of the song.

The hymn's melody is pentatonic—containing only five pitches. If the children are able to sing this hymn confidently, omit the accompaniment and try singing the hymn as a two- or even three-part canon, entering at the interval of one measure. This gives a totally different sound to the hymn and is fun to do.

Other Ideas:
• Use the Orff accompaniment. This accompaniment will also work with the canon idea above.
• Take the time to discuss the text to this hymn. Connect specific events in the life of Christ to the theme words and phrases found in the text.
• Consider asking someone to sing the first portion of each stanza as a solo, with the group joining at the pickup to measure 5. The song is sung in this manner on the *FaithSongs* CD.
• Sing selected stanzas as service music during Eastertide. Use stanza 1 or 3 as a response to the prayer; stanza 2 as a response to the confession of sins; stanza 4 as a part of your communion liturgy; and stanza 5 as a response to the benediction.

(JH)

Mary Told the Good News

The Resurrection of Jesus was truly "good news" for the women who visited the tomb. The angel told the women to "Go quickly and tell his disciples that he has risen from the dead." Read this account in Matthew 28:5-10.

Clap this pattern:

Speak the pattern as seen in measure 4: "Je-sus lives!" Locate other examples of this rhythm.

Clap the refrain. Divide the choir into two groups and clap the refrain in a two-part round. You may divide the choir into more groups. For more fun, give each group a different rhythm instrument.

Other Ideas:
• Use this song as a call to worship on Easter.
• Stanzas 2 and 3 are appropriate anytime during the Sundays between Easter and Pentecost.
• Sing the refrain and stanza 3 as a benediction.

(GW)

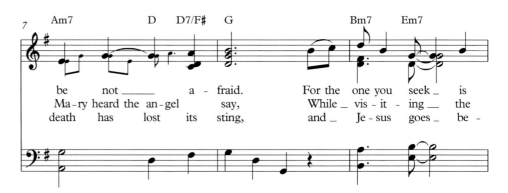

Anthem Setting: "Mary Told the Good News" by John D. Horman (Abingdon Press, 072255). Two-part treble voices and keyboard with optional handbells and Orff instruments.

The refrain may be sung as a round.

WORDS: John D. Horman
MUSIC: John D. Horman
© 1993 Abingdon Press, admin. by The Copyright Co., Nashville, TN 37212

God's Story • Easter and Eastertide

This Is the Day

Refrain

This is the day that the Lord _ has _ made! Re - joice! Re - joice, and

be ex - ceed - ing glad! This is the day that the Lord _ has _ made! Re -

joice! Re - joice! Hal - le - lu – jah!
1. Christ has con - quered
2. Je - sus lives who

death at last, left the tomb that held him fast!
once was dead, crown of glo - ry on his head.

Gone the sor - row, gone the night. Dawns the morn - ing clear and bright!
Ris - en now our Lord and King: songs of glad - ness let us sing.

WORDS: Natalie Sleeth
MUSIC: Natalie Sleeth
© 1976 Hinshaw Music, Inc. Used with permission.

God's Story • Easter and Eastertide

This song pairs the text of Psalm 118:24 with the Gospel accounts of Jesus' Resurrection. While many children may recognize these texts individually, they will especially enjoy seeing them working together in this cheerful song, especially if the text to Psalm 118:24 is used regularly in your worship setting as a call to worship or greeting.

See "Go Now In Peace" for information on the composer, Natalie Sleeth (page 90).

Begin by chanting the rhythm of the refrain text. Ask the children how many times they say "This is the day" to help them remember the form of the refrain.

Add body percussion using the rhythm of the Orff accompaniment written by John Horman (see below). Use alternating thigh pats (patschen) on the quarter notes and claps on the half notes. You may want to move hands in outward circles after each clap to give a sense of the duration of the half note.

Sing together the first and second phrases of the stanza and then the third and fourth phrases of the stanza. Ask the children, "Are these the same or different?" (The melody of the last measure of the second and fourth phrases are different.)

Other Ideas:
• Use the refrain as an antiphon with the verses of Psalm 118, as the call to worship or greeting for worship.
• This makes a great starter to gather your children together at the beginning of a rehearsal or class session.
• Use the Orff accompaniment below.

(DT)

God Sends Us the Spirit

The words of this song were written especially for this Gonja folk song from the African country of Ghana. Gonja is a state in the country of Ghana. Tom Colvin was one of the first persons to share the music of the African Christians with the rest of the world.

Play the first measure melody on step bells or the piano. This melodic fragment with a downward movement is the basis for the entire song. Ask the singers to find similar places in the remaining phrases of the song.

Teach the melody by playing it on the step bells so the singers can see the overall descending nature of the tune. Older singers can probably play the melody on the bells or tuned Orff instruments after only a few hearings.

An easy movement exercise for this song is to assign short running steps to the eighth notes and walking steps to the quarter notes. When you reach the words "Spirit friend" (measure 6), tell the children to kneel and fold hands.

Other Ideas:
- Use the Orff-style accompaniment.
- Add simple maracas and claves parts to enhance the song.
- This song would make a very effective Pentecost processional. Children could lead the line dance mentioned above down the aisles of the church.
- Discuss the various degrees of friendship with the children and how they are different. Ask: What kinds of friends do you have? How are they different? What is a best friend? What is a "Spirit-friend"? Why is the "S" capitalized?

(JH)

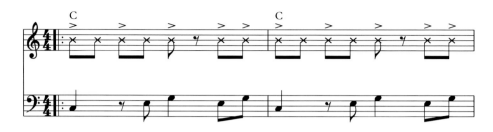

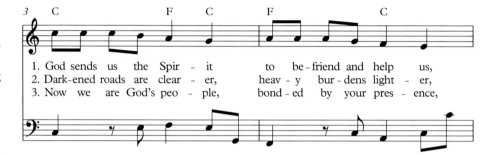

1. God sends us the Spir - it to be-friend and help us,
2. Dark-ened roads are clear - er, heav - y bur - dens light - er,
3. Now we are God's peo - ple, bond - ed by your pres - ence,

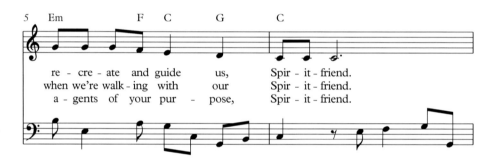

re - cre - ate and guide us, Spir - it - friend.
when we're walk - ing with our Spir - it - friend.
a - gents of your pur - pose, Spir - it - friend.

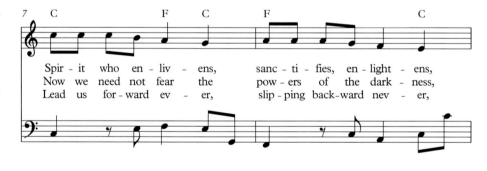

Spir - it who en - liv - ens, sanc - ti - fies, en - light - ens,
Now we need not fear the pow - ers of the dark - ness,
Lead us for - ward ev - er, slip - ping back-ward nev - er,

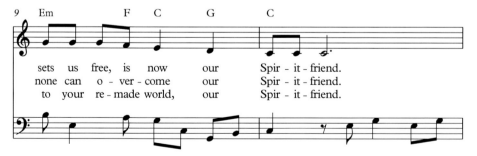

sets us free, is now our Spir - it - friend.
none can o - ver - come our Spir - it - friend.
to your re - made world, our Spir - it - friend.

WORDS: Tom Colvin
MUSIC: Gonja folk song, adapt. by Tom Colvin

God's Story • Pentecost

This lively chorus will be easily learned by your singers and congregation. The refrain–verse–refrain form is grasped easily.

There are only five different pitches in this song, D, E, F#, G, A. Drawing a staff on the chalkboard or chart paper with those notes will help in the learning of the tune.

Caution children against harsh singing on this song. The song's key and rhythm may lead children to oversing it (heavy and loud). Remind the children that they should sing "no louder than lovely." They will find that amusing, but they will remember it.

After the children can sing the main melody well, try adding a few voices to the descant. It's not a difficult descant but will require children who can sing a different higher melody without being distracted by the lower melody.

Other Ideas:
• Ask someone from the community to teach the children sign language for the refrain.
• This song is easy enough to be considered as cyclic song for Sunday worship. Cyclic songs are ones that are easily repeated while rituals or visual activities are being experienced by a congregation. If Communion is being served on Pentecost, this would be a good song for children to introduce to the congregation.
• Children will be able to easily add the D, E, F#, G, and A to this song on Orff-style barred instruments or choir chimes.
• This song can be used as a responsive antiphon between verses of scripture from the Pentecost story, after groups of prayers of concern, or as a litany response during the Pentecost season.

(JH)

Spirit, Come Down

106

WORDS: Janet Vogt and Mark Friedman
MUSIC: Janet Vogt and Mark Friedman

God's Story • Pentecost

All Night, All Day/Chatter with the Angels

Slaves coming to the Americas from Africa lived in such oppressive conditions that they often sang about the day when death would carry them to a happier place where the burdens of slavery were gone and hope and peace would abound. In both of these songs, joining a band of angels offered that vision of freedom.

Teach both parts to your singers, and then assign a specific part to each half. Begin by having the two groups face away from each other as they sing.

"Chatter with the Angels": Listen to the melody each time "chatter with the angels" occurs. How many times does it happen? (Six.) Is the tune always the same? (No.) How many different tunes do you hear with those words? (Two.) Can you learn both tunes and sing them at the right times in the song?

"All Night, All Day": Listen and sing together the four long notes that make up the opening idea. Ask the children to trace the "shape" of that short melodic segment in the air with the palm of their hand.

Other Ideas:

- Another Orff possibility: Set the barred instruments up in G pentatonic (no C's and F's); whenever the word "angel" is sung, the players can play any bars they choose. Metal barred instruments follow "All Night, All Day"; wooden instruments follow "Chatter with the Angels."

- Do you know other African American spirituals in which angels are mentioned? ("The Angel Band," "Swing Low, Sweet Chariot.")

(JH)

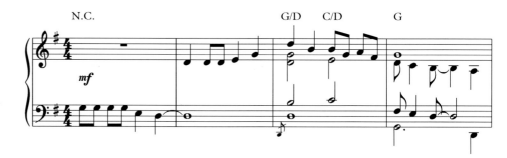

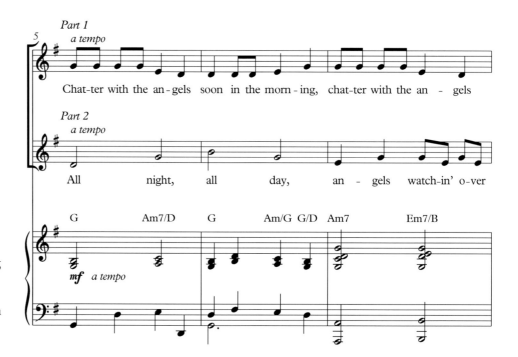

WORDS: African American spiritual
MUSIC: African American spiritual, arr. by John D. Horman
Arr. © 2003 Abingdon Press, admin. by The Copyright Co., Nashville, TN 37212

Orff Instruments

Jesus is known by many names in the Scriptures. Each name reveals something about the character of Christ. Ask the children to list names they know for Jesus and write their responses on the board. (Save this list for possible use for additional stanzas.)

Look at the song text and read each name. Discuss the meaning of each name in relation to Christ's nature.

The first two phrases are closely related. Teach these two phrases and have the children identify what is similar and different.

Write these five notes on a card or the board:

Play this pattern, then sing on "doo." Define and demonstrate the flat and natural symbols. Locate this pattern in the music, measures 9-12 ("Jesus . . . O") and sing.

Other Ideas:
- Add the hand claps as indicated in the score. You may choose to play these on rhythm instruments.
- Create and sing additional stanzas based on the list generated by the children in the opening discussion.
- Sing at informal gatherings, such as Sunday school, VBS, and church camp. This may be used as a call to worship or gathering song.

(GW)

He Is the King of Kings

*Hand claps or rhythm instruments.

WORDS: Virgil Meares
MUSIC: Virgil Meares

© 1989 Integrity's Hosanna! Music/ASCAP. c/o Integrity Media, Inc., 1000 Cody Rd., Mobile, AL 36695

God's Church • Celebration

Ho-Ho-Ho-Hosanna

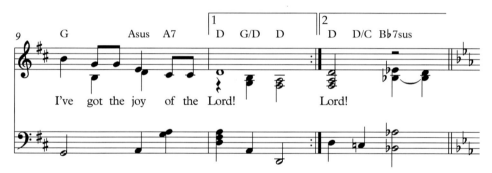

"Hosanna" and "hallelujah" are two words we sing many times throughout the church year. We begin singing them as preschool children and we are still singing them in our retirement years. Yet they are two of the most mispronounced words that we sing.

Make large cards labeled with the following colors: Yellow, Aqua, Red, Blue. The vowels in these words help singers to pronounce "hosanna" and "hallelujah" correctly:

Ho-	(yell**ow**)
san-	(**a**qua)
na	(aqu**a**)
Hal-	(**a**qua)
le-	(r**e**d)
lu-	(bl**u**e)
jah	(aqu**a**)

Other motions can help:

Ho-ho-ho: Use both hands to create a big "O" or circle in front of the mouth.

Ha-ha-hal: Hold straight hands vertically in front of the mouth for the tall "AH" sound.

He-he-he: Draw whiskers from your cheeks so that the sound is going toward the resonating chambers.

When you sing "the joy of the Lord," flip your fingers high in the air so that the joy and the sound spin in the air.

Other Ideas:

• This song is a great vocal exercise. Discuss good breath support with your singers. They should feel their stomachs pulsing as they sing "Ho-ho-ho" and "Ha-ha-hal."

• How many different musical elements can you add to this piece? *Forte, piano,* fast, slow, *staccato, legato.* Experiment!

(KE)

WORDS: Anon.
MUSIC: Anon.

God's Church • Celebration

Rock and roll with a new twist! Let's have some fun. Get out your bandanas, poodle skirts, sunglasses, ball caps, Hula Hoops® and Boomwhackers™! If you don't have Boomwhackers, you can substitute handchimes or keyboard playing the chords or singles notes of G, C, and D.

Hand motions can be added:

JESUS   Sign language sign
ROCK   Using closed fists, strike the right on top of the left
ROLLS   Make rolling motion with hands
AWAY   Flip the finger tips in the air

This is a fun song to use anytime your rehearsal or class needs a lift. In the midst of the fun, use this to encourage speaking/singing consonants together. Snap or tap on the quarter note as you say the text, listening together for the consonants.

(KE)

Jesus

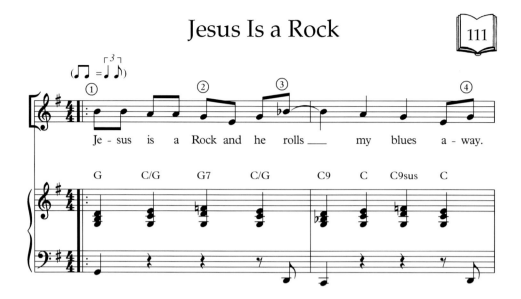

1. *Sign for Jesus.*
2. *Pound fists, one on top of the other.*
3. *Roll hands over each other.*
4. *Flip fingertips in the air.*
5. *Pass hands over each other, right on top for two beats, then left on top two beats, then right on top two beats.*
6. *Make "jazz" hands.*

WORDS: Tony Congi
MUSIC: Tony Congi

This setting combines three spirituals into a triple-partner song relationship. When each part is secure, your group will enjoy singing them together.

Beat is central to this song. March the pulse as the accompaniment is played. Vary the marching pulse using whole, half, quarter or eighth notes to discover the relationship of note values. Use a hand drum to illustrate the desired pulse.

Help your singers practice the difference in the rhythms between measures 4 and 8 by saying the word "hallelujah" several times, each time putting the accent on a different syllable of the word. Ask the singers to listen to the two "hallelujahs" in those measures as you sing them or play the CD. Discuss how they are different and practice saying them as you tap the beat on the hand drum.

Add motions and instruments to each song.

- Guide My Feet: Step right, touch left, step left, touch right with wood block.

- I Got Shoes: Patsch–snap–snap with hand drum.

- I'm Trampin': Clap with tambourine.

Other Ideas:
- Optional accompanying instruments, such as a drum set and bass may be used in place of the motion instruments listed above.
    Drum: Swing eighths
    Bass: Follow bass line of the accompaniment

Marchin' to the Beat of God

112

WORDS: African American spiritual; adapt. by John D. Horman
MUSIC: African American spiritual; arr. by John D. Horman
Adapt. and arr. © 2000 Abingdon Press, admin. by The Copyright Co., Nashville, TN 37212

• Sing this for a year-end choir recognition service; a casual church gathering, such as Wednesday night supper; or general anthem on serving God.

(GW)

Anthem Setting: "Marchin' to the Beat of God" by John D. Horman (Abingdon Press, 099730). Three-part equal voices and piano.

tramp - in', __ tryin' to make heav-en my home!

run this race in vain. _____

heav - en, __ heav - en, __ heav - en! __

Bb F2/A Gm7 Gm7/C Gm7/C F2/A Bb/C F

Rock-a My Soul

Discuss the Bible story of the rich man and Lazarus (Luke 16:19-31). Tell the children that Abraham is considered the founder of the Hebrew nation and the one to whom God made a covenant or promise (Gen. 17:4-8).

Explain that "the bosom of Abraham" is a Jewish symbol of blessedness after death. It also means a loving, safe place or a place close to one's heart. The text of the refrain refers to one's entrance into the place of rest. "You gotta go in at the door" means that you can only enter into "the bosom of Abraham" by God's grace through faith in Christ.

Use the song to teach about the origin/tradition of spirituals.

Other Ideas:
• Create a simple body ostinato on beats 2 and 4, such as clapping or snapping.
• Try these motions on the refrain:

"So high you can't get over it" Starting at waist level, raise hands over head, palms up.

"So low you can't get under it" Lower hands to waist level, palms down.

"So wide you can't get 'round it" Cross wrists and move hands outward in a sweeping motion.

"You gotta go in at the door" Quickly bring palms together and at chest level, move hands in a straight line forward, pulsing the hands on each beat (as if one is walking forward through the door).

(NB)

WORDS: Genesis 22; adapt. by Hal H. Hopson
MUSIC: African American spiritual; arr. by Hal H. Hopson
© 1993 Choristers Guild

God's Church • Celebration

Ministers, teachers, musicians, volunteers in the kitchen, volunteers who keep the church lawn, and many others are all part of the body of the church.

As a fun activity song, your group may never need to learn and memorize all the words to this song. The leader can sing it, with the children adding the motions and spoken words in the B section. Over time, the singers will pick up the words and join the leader.

Invent motions for "ah-choo," "listen up," "hey, look!" and "Good news!" Leave out (resting) the name of the body part and just do the motions.

When you repeat, don't forget to get faster. The last time, sing *a cappella* as fast as possible.

Other Ideas:
• Draw the outline of a body on a large poster or wall. From paper or posterboard, cut out the body parts that are used in the song. Take pictures of the many helpers at your church and attach them to the various body parts. While the group is singing the song, have some of the children attach the pictures/body parts to the outline.

(KE)

The Body Song

116

WORDS: Ann Wamberg
MUSIC: Ann Wamberg
© 1994 HarvestHarmonies. All rights reserved. Used by permission.

God's Church • Celebration

ears, *(Lis - ten up!)* some are eyes, *(Hey, look!)* some are

mouths, *(Good News!)* some are arms, *(hug, hug)* some are hearts, I love you.

rit. molto D.S.

⊕ CODA

do? Oh, __ with - out each part what would we

do? Oh __ with - out each part what would we do?

Talk about the importance of praising, loving, serving, and thanking Jesus throughout the day, not just during isolated moments. As believers in Jesus, we are to show our love for him at all times. Our very lives are to reflect his goodness.

Create a body ostinato, such as patsch (tap thighs), clap, patsch, clap. Vary the ostinato from verse to verse.

Create a rhythmic ostinato using percussion instruments, such as rhythm sticks, claves, tambourine, hand drums, and so on.

Other Ideas:
- Encourage the children to add their own stanzas.
- Use during the beginning of a rehearsal, assembly, or worship service.
- Works well with guitar only.
- Add simple motions, or sign the following words: JESUS, PRAISE, LOVE, SERVE, THANK

(NB)

Jesus

Praise

Love

Serve

Thank

Jesus in the Morning

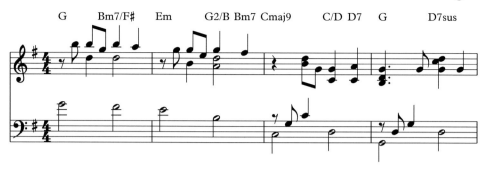

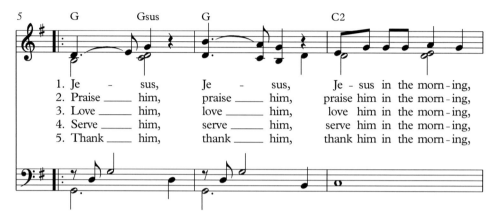

1. Je - sus, Je - sus, Je - sus in the morn-ing,
2. Praise ___ him, praise ___ him, praise him in the morn-ing,
3. Love ___ him, love ___ him, love him in the morn-ing,
4. Serve ___ him, serve ___ him, serve him in the morn-ing,
5. Thank ___ him, thank ___ him, thank him in the morn-ing,

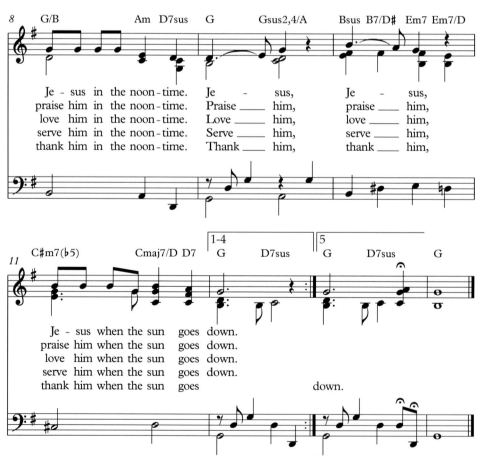

Je - sus in the noon-time. Je - sus, Je - sus,
praise him in the noon-time. Praise ___ him, praise ___ him,
love him in the noon-time. Love ___ him, love ___ him,
serve him in the noon-time. Serve ___ him, serve ___ him,
thank him in the noon-time. Thank ___ him, thank ___ him,

Je - sus when the sun goes down.
praise him when the sun goes down.
love him when the sun goes down.
serve him when the sun goes down.
thank him when the sun goes down.

WORDS: Traditional
MUSIC: Traditional

God's Church • Celebration

With My Voice

118

WORDS: Joyce Griffitts
MUSIC: Joyce Griffitts

This lyric very clearly states the four primary ways we use our voices: talking, whispering, singing, shouting. Here is a short poem to include with the song:

> I can talk! I can sing! I can whisper! I can shout!
> That's what my voice is all about!
> When I'm loud or I'm soft, Jesus hears me just the same!
> Let me use my voice in Jesus' name!

Explain the musical symbols: *f* (*forte*) means loud and *p* (*piano*) means soft. Ask the singers, "Which way to use your voice would match these musical dynamic markings?" Create small charts of the music symbols and show them at various times during the song as a music skill game.

Teach the "With my voice" three-note idea first. It happens three times. Which two are the same? (The first and second.) How is the third different from the first two? (It is higher.) Ask the children to sing "With my voice" and you complete the line. Later, after the children have learned the song, choose children to sing the "With my voice" sections as solos.

(JH)

Our church music heritage is rooted in the worship of the Levites of the Old Testament (1 Chron. 15:16; 2 Chron. 5:12-13). The refrain is based on Psalm 118:24. Singing the psalm refrain connects us to the sounds of the Levite singers in Temple worship.

Teach the refrain, noting that the first two phrases are identical. Teach the stanzas, noting similar musical phrases. With older students, note the text painting at "sky" as the melody ascends. Discover how text painting is used at this point in other stanzas, such as "lift your hands to the sky" and "ring them low, ring them high."

Other Ideas:

- This general anthem may be used as the first anthem of the year to kick off the fall or as the final anthem of the choir year, bringing together voices and instruments. Individual choirs may sing the stanzas with all joining on the refrain.
- Sing stanza 1 or the entire anthem as a call to worship.
- Sing the refrain as an antiphon to Psalm 118 or a similar praise psalm.
- Memorize Psalm 118:24.
- Create your own stanzas. Replace "singing" and "lifting a song to the sky" with suggestions from the choir. Add appropriate movements to accompany your new text.

(GW)

Now Is the Time

118

Anthem Setting: "Now Is the Time" by John Horman (Abingdon Press, 503604). Unison voices, instruments, and keyboard.

WORDS: John D. Horman
MUSIC: John D. Horman
© 1995 Abingdon Press, admin. by The Copyright Co., Nashville, TN 37212

God's Church • Music and Singing

joice! Re - joice and be glad _ in it!

G/D   Am9 Bm7 Cmaj7 C/D   G

Motions and Instruments

Stanza 2

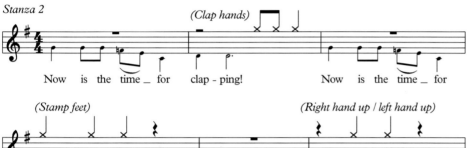

(Clap hands)

Now is the time _ for clap - ping! Now is the time _ for

(Stamp feet)   *(Right hand up / left hand up)*

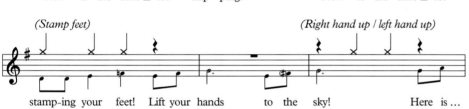

stamp-ing your feet! Lift your hands to the sky! Here is …

Stanza 3

(Crash cymbals or finger cymbals)

Now is the time _ for cym - bals! Now is the time _ for

(Snare drum or hand drum)   *(Crash cymbals or finger cymbals)*

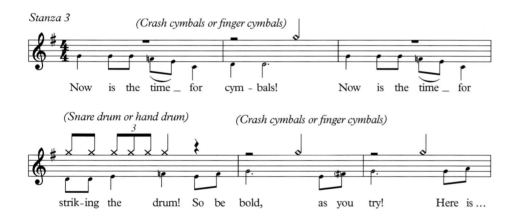

strik-ing the drum! So be bold, as you try! Here is …

Stanza 4

(Handbells)

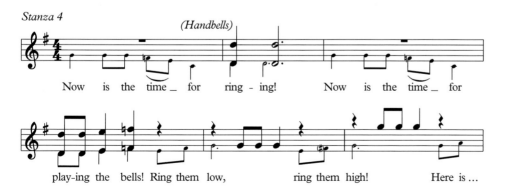

Now is the time _ for ring - ing! Now is the time _ for

play-ing the bells! Ring them low, ring them high! Here is …

The concept of faith, or belief, is foundational to our relationship with Jesus Christ. Throughout scripture, faith serves as the basis for salvation. From the time of Abraham (Gen. 15:6) through the Pauline Epistles and into the book of Revelation, faith precedes salvation.

Read Hebrews 11 to see how steadfast faith has guided those before us and will continue to be our lifeline. Hebrews 11 defines faith, and in this song, Hebrews 11:1 is echoed in the final phrase. Create a poster using the Hebrews 11:1 text. Invite the singers to memorize this text as you learn the song.

The opening four phrases give examples of how we may experience faith in our life. List these examples on the board and have the choir give a "real life" account for each.

Other Ideas:
- For a simple anthem, have a soloist or small group sing the song through once, then the entire choir sings the song.
- Sing this as an anthem for a children's ministry service or Children's Sabbath (second Sunday in October).
- Use the final phrase as an antiphon repeated several times during a reading of Hebrews 11. Use readers of various ages.
- This may serve as a year-long theme song for choir or Sunday school.
- Create an extended arrangement by repeating the song or singing the final phrase again. The example on the *FaithSongs* CD repeats the final phrase as a possible extended ending.

(GW)

Anthem Setting: "Faith" by Terry Kirkland (Abingdon Press, 502128). Unison voices and piano with optional descant.

Faith

WORDS: Terry Kirkland
MUSIC: Terry Kirkland

God's Church • Faith and Trust

God. _____ For faith is the sub-stance of

D   D   Em7   F♯m

things hoped for,   the ev - i-dence of things not seen.

Em/D   D   Em7   A   D

We Must Be Faithful

By examining the lives of Noah, Sarah, Moses, and Mary, we see how others have faithfully responded to God's call. How can we be obedient, faithful servants today?

Review this pattern:

Challenge the children to locate this pattern in the song. Note that the pattern occurs on different beats in different measures.

Other Ideas:

- Younger children sing the refrain and older children sing the stanzas, either as solos or in small groups.
- Alternate the refrain with speakers telling the biblical stories and stories of contemporary faithfulness.
- Use the song as an example of major and minor tonalities. The refrain is in G major and the stanzas are in G minor.
- Read and discuss the faithfulness of Noah (Gen. 6:13-22); Sarah (Gen. 18:11-14; 21:2); Moses (Exod. 14:21-29); and Mary (Luke 2:26-38).
- Ask older children to scan Hebrews 11 and create a list of the names mentioned and what each did in obedience to God.
- Sing this as a general anthem when Hebrews 11 or "faithfulness" is a service theme; or as a response to the sermon, such as an anthem of commitment.
- Teach the refrain to the congregation and direct them to join the children in singing the final refrain
- To create an extended instrumental ending, play measures 1-4 again and the 5th ending G chord.

(GW)

WORDS: Hebrews 11, adapted
MUSIC: John D. Horman

God's Church • Faith and Trust

18

warn-ing from a - bove, and built a might - y _____
she was ver - y old. God gave _ her _ a _
sea _ with his hand; al - low - ing _ God's _
bore _ God's true son, a child _ sent from _

Ebmaj7   Dm7   Gsus   G   G7   Cm7   Eb/F

21   *poco rit.*   5

ves - sel to sail through the flood. day.
son _ to love and to hold.
peo - ple to flee Pha - raoh's band.
heav - en to save ev - ery - one.

Dm7 Bb/D   Ebmaj7 Cm Am7   D9sus   D9 | 5
                                              | G

poco rit.

Anthem Setting: "We Must Be Faithful"
by John D. Horman (Abingdon Press,
034582). Unison and piano, with
optional descant, two-octave handbells,
and congregation.

God's Church • Faith and Trust

Children are able to trust without question—just as God has asked of us all. Read through the words of this song with the choir and identify elements of our relationship with God. Create a list on a poster to display in the room as you learn this song. Read Psalm 56:9-11 and Hebrews 2:13 for examples of trusting in God.

This melody consists of five four-measure phrases. Draw the melodic contour of each of these on the board.

As you echo-sing on an "oo" vowel, move your finger along the contour lines. Have the singers draw the contour in the air in front of them.

Light head tones are beautiful and healthy for the singing voice. Singing on the "oo" vowel helps place the tone. When the singers use text, ask them to strive for the same light singing sound. Continue to use the melodic contour lines to remind the singers to sing *legato* (smoothly).

Other Ideas:
• Ask the singers to identify which of the phrases are similar.
• Use "Love God with Your Heart" (page 64) as an scriptural introduction to this song. Change the last chord from G minor to G major and move directly into this song.
• Sing in worship with themes on trust, God's sovereignty, and general services.
• Use stanza 2 for stewardship themes.

(GW)

Song selected and adapted from *Showdown at Dry Gulch* by Henry Hinnant (Abingdon Press, 2001). Leader/Accompanist Edition, 0687016143.

1. Trust the Lord with all you are;
2. Trust the Lord with all your needs;
3. Though it seems im-prob-a-ble,

love the Lord with all your heart, and _____ you'll be a-
God pro-vides most gen-erous-ly. Nev-er de-ny that
God can make it pos-si-ble. God's strength be-gins when it

mazed what God can do through you.
God will in-deed pro-vide for you.
seems that your own is at an end.

WORDS: Henry Hinnant
MUSIC: Henry Hinnant

Wor - ship God through all your days, of - fer - ing un -
Sim - ple things that we pos - sess in God's hands are
Pray with faith and you will know God, in - deed, is

ceas - ing praise.
lim - it - less. God will be-come your strength and your song; God
in con - trol.

will be-come your sal - va - tion. For the Lord is my

God, and I'll sing prais - es. God, the _

Lord is my God, the _ Lord is my

God, and I'll sing prais - es.

God's Church • Faith and Trust

When I Am Afraid

When I am a-fraid, I will trust in you, I will trust in you, I will trust in you. When I am a-fraid, I will trust in you, in God, whose word I praise, God, whose word I praise. In God I trust when I am a-fraid, in God I trust, in God, whose word I praise.

All people, both children and adults, have fears. Share with the children something that frightens you and then ask them to share something that makes them feel afraid. Discuss God's willingness to help us and be with us when we are afraid.

Teach the form of the song and explain the meaning of ending 1, ending 2, and *Fine*.

Sing and clap the first two measures and have the children echo ("When I am afraid, I will trust in you"). Then sing measures 5-6 in the same way. Ask the children if the two phrases are the same or different and why. Follow the same procedure for the two measures of ending 1 and ending 2 ("in God, whose word I praise").

To help the children feel the beat in the second ending ("in God I trust"), have them tap the beat on their thighs (patschen) while they sing the melody. You can echo-sing and tap this section in two-measure phrases. Discuss how many beats each half note and dotted half note receives. Add snaps on the quarter note rests to help place the final consonants.

Other Ideas:
- Use this song as a companion song with "Be Still and Know" (page 58).
- Use in conjunction with a variety of Bible stories that deal with facing fear, such as the Exodus account; Daniel in the lion's den; David and Goliath; and Shadrach, Meshach, Abednego in the fiery furnace.

(NB)

WORDS: Frank Hernandez; based on Psalm 56:3-4a
MUSIC: Frank Hernandez; arr. by Emily R. Brink
© 1990 Birdwing Music/ASCAP. All rights admin. by EMI Christian Music Publishing.

God's Church • Faith and Trust

Fruit of the Spirit

Use this piece to introduce a study on the fruit of the spirit (see Galatians 5:22-26). Read this scripture to the children before introducing the song.

Plan to take several sessions to talk about each fruit: LOVE, JOY, PEACE, PATIENCE, KINDNESS, GOODNESS, FAITHFULNESS, GENTLENESS, SELF-CONTROL. During each session, spend time learning the song and memorizing the words. Ask the children to snap their fingers on the half notes as they sing to help them feel the syncopation.

Help the children discover the form of the piece by singing measures 5-14. Tell them you are going to call this part of the song "A." Sing measures 16-32 and call this part of the song "B." Ask the children to look at the music and tell you what order the parts of the song are sung. (A-B-A) Share that this is a popular form (order) for many songs. Highlight to them other songs you are singing that share this form.

Other Ideas

• Using inexpensive mops and brooms, design puppets to represent the fruit of the spirit. The students could also make an appropriate puppet play backdrop. Using a script of your own creation or one found in other resources, prepare a puppet presentation for an assembly, church night supper, or talent show. Begin and end the puppet presentation with the singing of the song.

(KE)

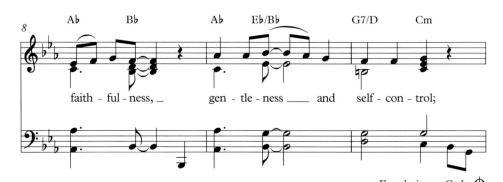

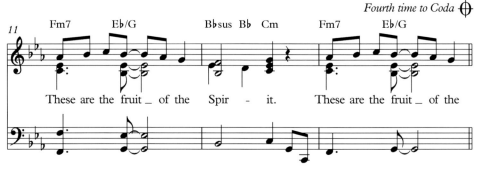

WORDS: Nancy Gordon and Chris Springer (based upon Galatians 5:22-26)
MUSIC: Nancy Gordon and Chris Springer

of the Spir - it in my life, I want the fruit ___

of the Spir - it shin-ing bright. ___ Je-sus,

take con - trol let your love o - ver-flow.

D.S. al Coda

I want the fruit _ of the Spir - it in my life. ___

CODA

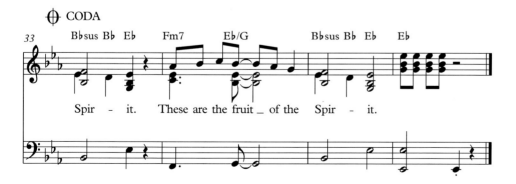

Spir - it. These are the fruit _ of the Spir - it.

Demonstrate with an oil lamp how oil is needed to keep the wick burning. We want to keep "burning" and praising at all times, even through the night, "till the break of day."

Talk with the children about how we need joy in our hearts to keep praising, peace in our hearts to keep loving, and love in our hearts to keep serving.

The melody of the stanza is easy to teach through repetition.

Note the ascending tone downbeat of the refrain melody. This is shown in the descant part. This makes this descant easy to teach and to sing.

Other Ideas:
- Ask someone in your congregation who is familiar with square dancing to teach your group some simple movements. These work well with this song.
- Some of your singers may know additional stanzas to the song. Encourage them in singing the alternate text for your group.
- A soloist or small group can add the descant to the song. Handchimes or a C instrument could also play the descant.
- Use the refrain as a joyful processional on Palm Sunday, repeating it several times as the children enter waving palm branches. Encourage the congregation to sing with the children. Once the congregation is singing, add a small group and/or instruments on the descant.

(KE)

Give Me Oil in My Lamp

WORDS: Traditional
MUSIC: Traditional

God's Church • Witness and Service

What does it mean to follow Jesus? Mention that Christians in other parts of the world suffer for their beliefs; still, these people "have decided to follow Jesus."

Although we may not risk our lives to follow Jesus, Christ's call to follow is not without risk. What are some of the risks we take when we decide to follow Jesus? (Examples: We risk giving up our self-centeredness and focus on Jesus instead; we risk being misunderstood by those who don't follow Jesus, and so on.)

Contact several parents, youth, Sunday school teachers, and other leaders in your church and share with them your study of this song. Ask them to write a letter to the children telling them of a time when this person had to make a conscious decision to follow Jesus in their life. If you have enough volunteers, each child could receive their own letter or you may want to read the letters to all the children at the close of your sessions.

Other Ideas:
• "When Jesus Saw the Fishermen" (page 101) and "Two Fishermen" (page 98) make good companion songs.
• "I Have Decided to Follow Jesus" is appropriate for worship during Lent or any time when commitment to Christ is the theme. It could be used during prayer time, or as a response to scripture or the sermon.

(NB)

I Have Decided to Follow Jesus

128

1. I have de-cid-ed ___ to fol-low Je-sus, I have de-cid-ed ___ to fol-low Je-sus, I have de-cid-ed ___ to fol-low Jesus — no turn-ing back, ___ no turn-ing back.
2. The world be-hind me, ___ the cross be-fore me, the world be-hind me, ___ the cross be-fore me, no turn-ing back, ___ no turn-ing back.
3. Though none go with me, ___ still I will fol-low, though none go with me, ___ still I will fol-low — no turn-ing back, ___ no turn-ing back.

WORDS: Anon.
MUSIC: Anon., arr. by Eugene Thomas
Arr. © 1986 Word Music

Signing for "I've Got Peace Like a River" (page 175).

Peace   Joy   Love

God's Church • Witness and Service

I've Got Peace Like a River

1. I've got peace like a riv-er, I've got peace like a riv-er, I've got peace like a riv-er in my soul. I've got peace like a riv-er, I've got peace like a riv-er, I've got peace like a riv-er in my soul.

2. I've got joy like a foun-tain, I've got joy like a foun-tain, I've got joy like a foun-tain in my soul. I've got joy like a foun-tain, I've got joy like a foun-tain, I've got joy like a foun-tain in my soul.

3. I've got love like an o-cean, I've got love like an o-cean, I've got love like an o-cean in my soul. I've got love like an o-cean, I've got love like an o-cean, I've got love like an o-cean in my soul.

WORDS: African American spiritual
MUSIC: African American spiritual

God's Church • Witness and Service

Ask the children what "peace like a river," "joy like a fountain," and "love like an ocean," mean to them. What feelings do these images convey? Does our relationship with God fill us with peace, joy, and love? If so, when we are filled with these gifts from God, how does it affect our behavior?

Create a piece of art inspired by the images of these stanzas. Display the art in a highly visible location so the congregation can enjoy it.

If you have a strong soloist in your group, consider letting the soloist sing the first verse, with the group joining on verse 2. Because the song comes from an oral tradition, encourage the soloist (and the group, at least in rehearsal) to improvise.

Other Ideas:
- Develop simple motions, or add sign language for the following words: PEACE, JOY, LOVE.
- Devise a simple, "on-the-beat" body ostinato, such as:
  1. Patsch (tap thighs), clap, tap shoulders, tap head, *or*
  2. Patsch, clap, snap, clap
  Allow different children to be the ostinato leader.
- The song is suitable for use in rehearsal, assemblies, and worship services. If part of a worship service, the song could be used as an act of praise or as a response to a prayer or sermon.
- Works well with keyboard and/or guitar, or worship band.
- Use the song to teach about the origin/tradition of spirituals.

(NB)

The image of Jesus as shepherd is common in Scripture. A shepherd cares for the sheep, seeing that they are fed and safe. A shepherd leads them to pastures that are green while fending off dangerous enemies. A shepherd calls the sheep by name, and they know their shepherd's voice. Read about our Shepherd in these scriptures: Psalm 23; 28:9; Isaiah 40:11; Ezekiel 34:11-15; Matthew 2:6; John 10:11-15; 1 Peter 2:25; and Revelation 7:17.

The stanza is easy to teach by having the children echo you. Use a child soloist or small group to sing measures 1–20 when they are familiar with the melody. Everyone sings measure 21 to the end.

Other Ideas:
- Ask someone who knows sign language in your community to sign this song as it is sung or invite them to teach the signs to the children.
- Ask a youth or adult who is experienced in dance to interpret the song through dance for the children.
- Create a medley with "The Lord Is My Shepherd" (page 70) or other settings of Psalm 23.
- Sing this in a variety of settings, such as Sunday school, vacation Bible school, or summer camp. Use as a call to commitment in worship or anytime the scriptures above are used.

(GW)

You Are My Shepherd

WORDS: Mary Rice Hopkins and Denny Bouchard
MUSIC: Mary Rice Hopkins and Denny Bouchard

God's Church • Witness and Service

The rainbow serves as a reminder of God's faithful covenant established with Noah. Read about the promise in Genesis 9:12-17. When we allow God's light to shine through us, we can become the "rainbow of God's love" to others. Look through the anthem text to discover ways we can serve as God's "rainbow."

Color a large rainbow to display in the classroom as you study this song. Remember "Roy G. Biv" (red, orange, yellow, green, blue, indigo, violet) for the color order.

Locate the rainbow melodic shape on the word "rainbow" at the end of the song. Sing this phrase, drawing a rainbow in the air as you sing this word.

Other Ideas:
• Read, then find the references to these stories in the song: Matt. 19:13-15 (children come to Jesus); Mark 12:41-44 (widow's mite); Matt. 20:29-34 (healing the blind); John 11:32-45 (raising of Lazarus); Matt. 15:29-31 (healing the lame); Gen. 17:15-22 (Abraham and Sarah bear a son); Jer. 1:4-10 (calling of Jeremiah); Luke 15:1-7 (lost sheep); and Matt. 8:14-17 (healing the sick).
• Ask someone from the community to teach sign language to the refrain.
• Sing this song when the emphasis is on Jesus' ministry, growing in Christ's image, or serving others.
• The refrain may be used as a benediction.

(GW)

Anthem Setting: "Rainbow of God's Love" by Daniel Burton (Abingdon Press, 027861). Unison voices and piano.

Rainbow of God's Love

WORDS: Daniel Burton
MUSIC: Daniel Burton

God's Church • Witness and Service

Children will enjoy this text, which identifies ways they can give praise to God. Look at the text and list the four things that can praise: hands, ears, eyes, and life.

Ask the children to list ways each thing can offer praise to God. Write their suggestions on the board.

Echo-sing stanza 1, signing "hands" each time it appears. Illustrate the melodic movement using the hands and body, step bells, or numbers/syllables on the board. Identify melodic leaps, isolating them for accuracy as needed.

Work on breath control. The song should have three long four-measure phrases in measures 5-16. Ask the children to pretend to smell a rose to get a sense of a correct, deep breath. Also, pretend to sip air in through a straw.

Other Ideas:
• Consult with someone who is proficient in signing to teach the sign language for this text.
• Simple motions for measures 1-8 and measures 17-22 could be created and easily learned since the text is almost the same for each stanza.
• Sing for worship with themes on stewardship or children's ministry.

(GW)

The Giving Song

1. Here are my hands, Lord, I give you
2. Here are my ears, Lord, I give you
3. Here are my eyes, Lord, I give you
4. Here is my life, Lord, I give you

praise. Teach them to serve you for all of my
praise. Teach them to lis - ten for all of my
praise. Teach them to seek you for all of my
praise. Help me to love you for all of my

days. Help them to stay ___ both faith - ful and
days. Help them to stay ___ both faith - ful and
days. Help them to stay ___ both faith - ful and
days. Help me to stay ___ both faith - ful and

WORDS: Pamela Martin
MUSIC: Joseph M. Martin
© 1996 McKinney Music, Inc. (BMI). All rights reserved. Used by permission.

God's Church • Witness and Service

true.   Here   are   my   hands,   Lord,
true.   Here   are   my   ears,   Lord,
true.   Here   are   my   eyes,   Lord,
true.   Here   is   my   life,   Lord,

I   give   them   to   you.
I   give   them   to   you.
I   give   them   to   you.
I   give   it   to   you.

The Sharing Song

Learning to share is part of our social and spiritual development. Children may understand sharing a toy before they comprehend sharing God's love. This song, based on Matthew 25:34-40, reminds us that when we share with those in need, we also share with Jesus.

The simple melody can be taught easily. Sing the song to the children. Invite them to hum the melody with you as you sing the text. They can move to singing the text when they are comfortable with the melody.

Other Ideas:
• Read and discuss Matthew 25:34-40.
• Sing the final four measures as a response to the assurance of pardon or as a benediction. Repeat several times and invite congregational participation.
• Add sign language to the refrain. Signs needed: GOD, LOVES, US/WE, SHARE
• Schedule a service activity for your choir.
• Sing as a response to a sermon based on Matthew 25:34-30; or when the theme is World Hunger Sunday, Crop Walk Sunday, social concerns, or servanthood.

(GW)

Anthem setting: "The Sharing Song" by Nylea L. Butler-Moore (Abingdon Press, 023890). Unison voices (optional obbligato instrument, guitar, and congregation) with piano.

WORDS: Based on Matthew 25:34-40
MUSIC: Nylea L. Butler-Moore
© 1995, 1998 Abingdon Press, admin. by The Copyright Co., Nashville, TN 37212

God's Church • Witness and Service

God

Loves

Us/We

Share

Not much is written about the origin of this song. There are many versions of it. It was originally passed from person to person through oral tradition. The song was popular long before it was officially written down in musical notation and text.

Ask the children if they know any other versions of this song. Explain that when a song is passed from person to person without being written down, something is bound to happen to the song. What do you think happens?

Form a circle and begin sending a message around the circle from person to person by whispering it into the next person's ear. Most of the children will be familiar with this game. What happens to the original message?

This is what happens to songs that are passed down by oral tradition. They undergo changes and alterations as people hear them a bit differently each time they are sung.

Using the chords written above the melody, add choir chimes or autoharp to this song. The chords can be simplified to three chords: C (C-E-G), F (F-A-C), and G7 (G-B-D-F.)

Other Ideas:
• This song is a good class ender or choir closer.
• It is also easy enough that once the children are all comfortable singing it, children will readily volunteer to sing it as a solo. Making up stanzas is also easy to do and children will enjoy doing this as an extra activity.

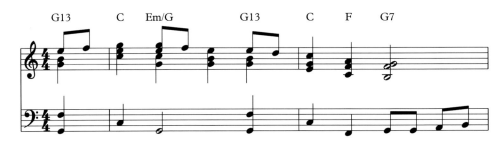

1. This lit-tle light of mine,   I'm gon-na let it shine!

This lit-tle light of mine,   I'm gon-na let it shine!   This lit-tle light of mine,

I'm gon-na let it shine! Let it shine, let it shine, let it shine!

2. Hide it un-der a bas-ket? No!   I'm gon-na let it shine.
3. Don't let an-y-one (blow) it out.   I'm gon-na let it shine.
4. Share my light _ with oth-ers! Yes!   I'm gon-na let it shine.

WORDS: Traditional
MUSIC: Traditional; arr. by David McDonald

13 **F** **F** **C** **G13**

Hide it un-der a bas-ket? No! I'm gon-na let it shine.
Don't let an-y-one *(blow)* it out. I'm gon-na let it shine.
Share my light _ with oth-ers! Yes! I'm gon-na let it shine.

• Some persons like to sing the text of stanza 1 as a refrain between stanzas 2, 3, and 4. You may want to consider this when singing with a choir and congregation to allow the congregation to join in the singing.

(JH)

15 **C** **C**

Hide it un-der a bas-ket? No! I'm gon-na let it shine,
Don't let an-y-one *(blow)* it out. I'm gon-na let it shine, } let it
Share my light _ with oth-ers. Yes! I'm gon-na let it shine,

17 **C/G** **Fmaj7/G G7** **1, 2** **C** **3** **C**

shine, let it shine, let it shine. shine.

God's Church • Witness and Service

This song derives its thematic material from the Beatitudes in the Sermon on the Mount (Matt. 5:9).

The song has a wonderful feeling of threes. It swings and bounces in sets of three beats per measure. The children can count those sets of threes while listening to the CD or to someone singing and playing it on the piano (123–123–123–123).

Add body percussion; patsch–clap–clap is a good way to experience that grand feeling of three.

You can also help the children feel the strong beat of a measure by bouncing balloons or waving crepe paper streamers. It's helpful to do a "pretend" version of this activity first so that the children understand it. Introduce it by demonstrating the action and asking if anyone can guess what it is—balloons bouncing or paper streaming. Each child may have their own balloon or you may want to partner the children or create smaller groups to tap a single balloon to the downbeat of each measure.

Other Ideas:
• Can the children name people from the last one hundred years who fall into the category of "peacemaker"? (Examples: Mahatma Gandhi, Martin Luther King, Jr., Jimmy Carter, mothers and fathers, and so on.)
• Use this song anytime the scripture lesson is on peace. Also consider using this song when your community is focusing on global, national, or local neighborhood peace.

(JH)

WORDS: Mark Burrows, alt.
MUSIC: Mark Burrows
© 2001 Abingdon Press, admin. by The Copyright Co., Nashville, TN 37212

Make Me a Servant

Jesus exemplified for us what being a servant means. He helped others who were ignored, forgotten, scorned. He served others when he, by right of being God's Son, should have been served himself.

John 13:14-16 relates the story of when Jesus washed his disciples' feet. The very act of washing someone's feet was an act of servanthood. Philippians 2:1-11 encourages us to imitate Christ's humility and to be in service to others. "Make Me a Servant" is a prayer asking God to help us be people who love and care for others in Jesus' name.

Use the song to teach the concepts of the musical phrase and deep breathing. Because each musical phrase is four measures long, good breaths and singing posture are needed.

Teach children where to place the "k" sound in "meek" and "weak" and to intensify the "k" sound in the word "make." Unify the vowel sound in the second syllable of the word "ser-vant" and work on unified placement of the "t."

Other Ideas:
- Consider using the song in conjunction with a mission activity or as a group "theme" song.
- This song can be used during prayer time, as a response to a scripture or sermon, or as a closing song.
- Works well with keyboard and guitar, or a worship band.

(NB)

WORDS: Kelly Willard
MUSIC: Kelly Willard

God's Church • Witness and Service

Da Pacem Domine
(Grant Us Peace, O Lord)

Words of peace and reconciliation are used in worship as a renewal of relationships with God and with one another. This simple text humbly asks God's peace to be with us at all times. Read John 14:27 to discover the peace that God offers us through Jesus Christ. Other scriptures offering peace include: 1 Samuel 25:6; Psalm 29:11; and 2 Corinthians 13:11.

Latin Pronunciation Guide:

da PAH-chehm
DOH-mee-neh
een dee-EH-boos
NOH-strees

Echo-sing by two-measure phrases. Part 2 may be sung or doubled on a C instrument, such as flute or recorder.

Other Ideas:

- The composer, César Franck (1822–1890) was Belgian-born but became a naturalized French citizen. He was a pianist and organist who specialized in church music and improvisation. Find out more about this composer at your library or on the Internet.
- Sing this as part of Taizé-style worship by repeating it several times as needed.
- Use in worship as a call or response to prayer; call to the passing of the peace; or as a benediction.
- Ask the children to sing one part and your adults to sing the other for an intergenerational experience.
- Create an anthem by singing the first part, moving to the second part, and then returning back to the first part. Consider singing the two parts together to create a final ending. The voices on the *FaithSongs* CD sing both parts together the final time.

WORDS: César Franck
MUSIC: César Franck; acc. by David L. Bone
Acc. © 2003 Abingdon Press, admin. by The Copyright Co., Nashville, TN 37212

(GW)

God's Church • Community of God

Walk with Me

138

Refrain

1. When Mo - ses heard the call of God he
2. Now Pe - ter was a most un - like - ly
3. Young Ma - ry Mag - a - lene was sure her
4. And when you share your faith with me and

said, "Lord, don't send me." But God told Mo - ses,
man to lead the flock; but Je - sus knew his
life could be much more, and by her faith she
work for life made new, the wit - ness of your

"You're the one to set my peo - ple free."
ho - li - ness and he be - came the Rock.
dared to let God's love un - lock the door.
faith - ful - ness calls me to walk with you.

Walk with me, I will walk with you and

build the land that God has planned where love shines through.

WORDS: John S. Rice
MUSIC: John S. Rice, arr. by David L. Bone
© 1988, 2003 The Estate of John S. Rice

God's Church • Community of God

When God calls us to a task, we are not alone. God promises to guide us in the fulfillment of that call. As you learn this song, invite your singers to name those who heard and obeyed God's call. They were faithful to God.

Invite all to walk the half note pulse as the leader chants the refrain in rhythm. Can the singers chant the refrain as they walk? Sing the refrain as you walk.

Ask a soloist to sing the stanzas as the choir stands still as if listening for God's call. Everyone sing the refrain as they walk around the circle.

Clap the rhythmic pattern of measure 9. This rhythm is used throughout the stanza. Ask the singers, "How many measures use this rhythm?" "Can you speak the text in rhythm each time it appears?" Sing the stanza, clapping this rhythm when it is used.

Other Ideas:
• To learn more, read Exodus 3:1–4:20; Matthew 16:13-20; and Mark 16:9. How did God use these people?
• Sing this song in worship with themes on God's call, discipleship, and commitment.
• You may choose to select soloists to sing stanzas 1-3, representing those who have been called. Have the entire choir join on the refrain and stanza 4.

(GW)

The text of this traditional Hebrew song can be translated "We bring you peace." Many children will be aware of the need for peace in the Middle East and around the world. Explore ways that your singers can create peace in their world.

Hebrew Pronunciation Guide:
Heh-VAY-noo shah-LOHM ah-LECH*-em
(*The "ch" is sounded as in the Germanic "Bach.")

Easy movements can be added.
Phrases 1 and 2:
Move in a circle, using a side step.
Phrase 3:
Move into the center, hands joined, raising your arms in praise.
Phrase 4:
Let go of hands in center, clap once with each "shalom," taking a step backward each time (three times) into the original circle.

Other Ideas:
• Add Orff ostinato.

(or handchimes played one octave lower)

• Sing this in worship during the passing of the peace; as a call to worship; or as a gathering song for Sunday school, choir rehearsal, vacation Bible school, camp, or other similar activity.

(GW)

WORDS: Traditional Hebrew
MUSIC: Traditional Hebrew, arr. by David L. Bone
Arr. © 2003 Abingdon Press, admin. by The Copyright Co., Nashville, TN 37212

Things We Do In Choir

Use the secret code below to find out some things we do in choir.

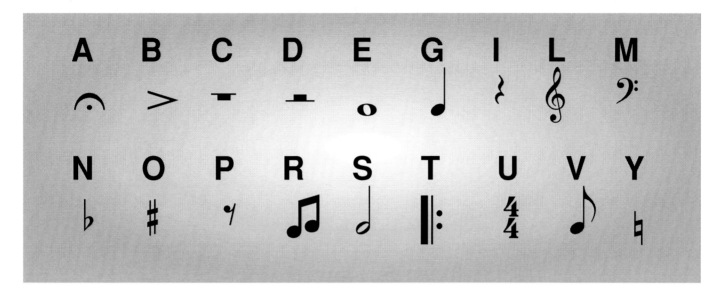

1. _____ _____

2. _____ _____

3. _____ _____

4. _____ _____

Though originally associated with the story of Daniel in the musical *Daniel's Dangerous Dilemma*, this song can offer voice to any occasion that looks forward to "a brand new day." The season of Advent is filled with these images, particularly from the book of Isaiah.

Create a mural or banner with a large world in the middle. Superimpose "bright faces" to represent a diversity of people (races, cultures, ethnic groups) on the world. All ages, or just children's faces, could be used. Use the text of the song for additional ideas.

Practice the large ascending interval leaps: perfect 4th (D to G), perfect 5th (D to A), and minor 7th (D to C). Visually isolate the intervals by writing them on a large staff. Ask the singers to imagine that they are vertically stretching a rubber band as they sing these intervals. When the children can sing the intervals in tune, ask them where the intervals occur in the song.

Other Ideas:
- This song would be appropriate for use during Advent, on Peace and Justice Sunday, World Communion Sunday, Human Relations Day, or any other day when peace and unity are the theme.
- Discuss the discipleship issues of loving, watching, and praying. How can positive changes within each person lead to the world being as one?

(NB)

Anthem Setting: "A Brand New Day" by Michael Bedford (Abingdon Press, 074207). Unison voices and keyboard with optional flute.

A Brand New Day

WORDS: Michael Bedford
MUSIC: Michael Bedford

God's Church • Community of God

Saints are identified by the lives they lead. Whether living or dead, saints often personify the characteristics of the Christian life. Recall those who are models to you as you teach about these faithful servants.

Invite the choir to identify the qualities of a saint as illustrated in the song. Write the list on a chalkboard. Name saints of old (St. Francis, St. Patrick, St. Valentine, St. Nicholas) and saints today (persons in your congregation or community).

Write the refrain on a large sheet of paper. Label each note using either numbers or solfège. Teach the refrain using the chart, singing either the numbers or solfège. Identify and demonstrate the octave leap.

Other Ideas:
- Learn the hymn "I Sing a Song of the Saints of God" as you learn this anthem.
- Sing this as a general anthem for All Saints Sunday. The refrain may be used as a response to the Gospel lesson or benediction in the same service.
- Use a "Scale Ladder" to visually show the rise and fall of the pitches of the melody and the octave leap. See "Other Ideas" on page 9 for directions.

Saints Today, Saints of Old

WORDS: John D. Horman
MUSIC: John D. Horman

God's Church • Community of God

- If you are using the *FaithSongs* CD, there are two measures added at the end of the refrain between stanzas 2 and 3 and between stanzas 4 and 5 to give your singers a chance to get a good breath between stanzas.

(GW)

Anthem Setting: "Saints Today, Saints of Old" by John D. Horman (Abingdon Press, 50161X). Unison voices (optional two-part and optional SATB) and piano.

God's Church • Community of God

FaithSongs
Children's Choir Rehearsal Planning Worksheet

Date _____ Choir _____

Preparation and Overview

Musical concepts in this rehearsal:

_____

_____

_____

Spiritual/worship concepts in this rehearsal:

_____

_____

_____

Activities to enhance learning of concepts:

_____

_____

_____

Preparation/supplies needed:

_____

_____

_____

1. Prerehearsal/arrival activities:

    a) _____

    b) _____

    c) _____

2. Opening prayer:

_____

_____

_____

3. Vocal warm-ups:

    a) _____

    b) _____

    c) _____

4. Anthems/hymns/songs for next worship service and related teaching plans:

_____

_____

_____

5. Music to continue learning for future services and related teaching plans:

_____

_____

_____

6. New material to be introduced and related teaching plans:

_____

_____

_____

7. Announcements:

_____

_____

_____

8. Devotional and closing prayer (led by _____):

9. Take home (reminders, handouts):

_____

_____

_____

_____

10. Comments:

Learning Event (Song/devotional/activity)	Leader's	Singer's	CD#/Track#	Goal
_____	_____	_____	_____	_____
_____	_____	_____	_____	_____
_____	_____	_____	_____	_____

Acknowledgments

Augsburg Fortress Publishers, PO Box 1209; Minneapolis, MN 55440-1209; (612) 330-3300

Big Steps 4 U (see Music Services)

Birdwing Music (ASCAP) (see EMI Christian Music Publishing)

Brentwood-Benson Music Publishing, Inc. (ASCAP); Attn: Commercial Licensing; 741 Cool Springs Blvd.; Franklin, TN 37067

Broadman Press (see Genevox Music Group)

Bud John Songs, Inc. (ASCAP) (see EMI Christian Music Publishing)

CCCM Music (see Maranatha! Music)

Cedarmont Music, LLC (ASCAP); PO Box 680145; Franklin, TN 37068-0145

Celebration; PO Box 309; Aliquippa, PA 15001; (724) 375-1510; FAX (724) 375-1138

Changing Church Forum, 200 E. Nicollet Blvd.; Burnsville, MN 55337; (800) 874-2044; FAX (952) 435-8015

Choristers Guild, 2834 W. Kingsley Rd., Garland, TX 75041; (972) 271-1521; FAX (972) 840-3113

Christian Conference of Asia, 96 Pak Tin Village, Meitin Road, Shatin, New Territories, Hong Kong, China; FAX (011) 8-52-2692-4378

CRC Publications, 2850 Kalamazoo Ave. SE, Grand Rapids, MI 49560; (800) 333-8300; FAX (888) 642-8606

David Dargle (see Choristers Guild)

Roger Day, PO Box 981, Franklin, TN 37065

EMI Christian Music Publishing, 101 Winners Circle, PO Box 5085, Brentwood, TN 37024; (615) 371-4300

Mark Friedman and Janet Vogt (see OCP Publications)

General Board of Global Ministries, GBGMusik, 475 Riverside Dr., Room 350, New York, NY 10115

Genevox Music Group, 127 Ninth Avenue North, Nashville, TN 37234; (800) 884-7712; FAX (615) 251-3727

GIA Publications, Inc., 7404 S. Mason Ave.; Chicago, IL 60638; (800) GIA-1358; FAX (708) 496-3828

Group Publishing, Inc., 1515 Cascade Ave., PO Box 481, Loveland CO 80539

HarvestHarmonies, FAX (719) 599-4573

Hinshaw Music, Inc., PO Box 470, Chapel Hill, NC 27514-0470; (919) 933-1691; FAX (919) 976-3399

Hope Publishing Company, 380 South Main Pl., Carol Stream, IL 60188; (800) 323-1049; FAX (630) 665-2552; www.hopepublishing.com

House of Mercy Music (see The Copyright Company)

Jane Parker Huber (see Westminster John Knox Press)

Integrity Media, Inc., 1000 Cody Road, Mobile, AL 36695

Integrity's Hosanna! Music/ASCAP (see Integrity Media, Inc.)

Integrity's Praise! Music (BMI) (see Integrity Media, Inc.)

W. L. Jenkins (see Westminster John Knox Press)

Les Presse de Taizé (see GIA Publications, Inc.)

Lillenas Publishing Company (see The Copyright Company)

Lutheran Book of Worship (see Augsburg Fortress Publishers)

McKinney Music, Inc. (BMI) (see Genevox Music Group)

Neil MacNaughton, 207 Salvator Blvd., Oakville, Ontario, Canada L6L 1N1

Make Way Music (see Music Services in the Western Hemisphere)

Maranatha! Music (see The Copyright Company)

Maranatha Praise, Inc. (see The Copyright Company)

Meadowgreen Music Company (ASCAP) (see EMI Christian Music Publishing)

Simei Montiero (see Choristers Guild)

Music Services, Inc. (ASCAP), 209 Chapelwood Dr., Franklin, TN 37069; (615) 749-9015; www.musicservices.org

New Spring Publishing, Inc. (ASCAP) (see Brentwood-Benson Music Publishing)

OCP Publications, 5536 NE Hassalo, Portland, OR 97213

Pilot Point Music (see The Copyright Company)

PsalmSinger Music (see The Copyright Company)

Sound III, Inc. (see Universal-MCA Music Publishing)

The Copyright Company, 1025 16th Ave. S., Suite 204, Nashville, TN 37212; FAX (615) 321-1099

The Estate of John S. Rice, 819 Sunnydale Rd., Knoxville, TN 37923

The Kruger Organization, Inc., 4501 Connecticut Ave., NW, Suite 711, Washington, DC 20008; (202) 966-3280; FAX (202) 364-1367

Tony Congi Music, 14 Honeysuckle Ct., Stormville, NY 12582

Universal-MCA Music Publishing, A Division of Universal Studios, Inc. (see Warner Bros. Publications U.S. Inc.)

Warner Bros. Publications U.S. Inc., 15800 NW 48th Ave., Miami, FL 33014-4340

Westminster John Knox Press, 100 Witherspoon St., Louisville, KY 40202; (502) 569-5342; FAX (502) 569-5113 ("Wonder of Wonders" is from A Singing Faith; "When Jesus Saw the Fishermen" is from Songs and Hymns for Primary Children)

WGRG (see GIA Publications, Inc.)

Whole Armor Music & Full Armor Music (see the Kruger Organization, Inc.)

Willing Heart Music (see The Copyright Company)

Word Music Group, 20 Music Square East, Nashville, TN 37203

Word Music, Inc. (see Word Music Group)

Darlene Zschech/Hillsong Publishing (see Integrity's Hosanna! Music)

Index of Scripture

Genesis
1	19, 20
6:13-22	164
9:12-17	178
15:6	162
17:4-8	154
18:11-14	164
21:2	164
22	154

Exodus
3:1–4:20	189
14:21-29	164
15:1-21	34
15:26	58
33:21-23	36

Deuteronomy
6:5	54, 64, 65, 66

1 Kings
19:11-13	58

Psalm
8	21, 46
18:2-3	26
19	33, 46
23	70, 176
31:14	58
46:10	58
56:3-4a	169
56:9-11	166
66	29
91:11-12	144
95:1	12, 52
98	52, 60
100	9, 24, 29
118:14	166
118:24	24, 139, 160
133	57, 59
134:1-2	62
139:7-10	71
148	46
150	30

Song of Solomon
8:6	78

Isaiah
6:3	77
7:14; 9:6	109
9:2	110
9:6, 7	21, 108
11:1, 6	110
40:3-5	110, 114
40:11	176
40:31	92
55:12-13	94

Matthew
2	118
2:1-12	117, 126
4:18-25	98, 101, 174
5:9	186
5:14-16	184
6:33	68
7:7	68
8:14-17	178
10:1-4	106
16:13-20	102, 189
19:13-15	113, 178
20:29-34	178
21:1-17	130, 134
21:8-9	114, 128
21:9-11	147
22:34-40	40, 54, 64, 65, 66
25:1-13	172
25:34-40	182
26:17-30	84
27:27-56	134
27:57-60	133
28:5-10	136, 138
28:19	82

Mark
1:16-20	98, 101, 174
3:13-18	106
10:13-16	113
11:1-10	130
11:8-10	114, 128, 147
11:15-19	134
12:28-34	40, 54, 64, 65, 66
14:12-26	84
14:17-50	134
15:43-46	133
16:6-7, 9	136, 189

Luke
1:46-47	116
2:1-7	124
2:1-20	117, 120
2:8-20	119, 123
2:14	56
2:29	90
5:1-11	98, 101, 174
8:1-3	98
10:25-28	40, 54, 64, 65, 66
16:12-16	106
16:19-31	154
18:15-17	113
19:29-38	114, 128, 130
22:7-20	84
23:50-53	133
24:1-9	164
24:5	136

John
1:1-2, 14, 18	124
1:40-42	98, 102, 174
3:16	127
8:12	184
10:11-15	176
11:32-45	178
12:12-13	114, 128
13:14-16	187
14:27a	96
19:38-42	133, 134
20:1-8	134
20:19-23	40

Acts
2:1-4	140
2:1-13	142
3:1-8	100
4:12	44
4:24-30	22

Romans
12:1	76

1 Corinthians
6:19	76
10:17	86
12:12-31	156
15:3-4	42

2 Corinthians
4:6	50

Galatians
5:22-26	170

Ephesians
6:23	90

Philippians
2:1-11	187
2:9-11	44
4:4	48

2 Thessalonians
3:16	90

Hebrews
2:13	166
11	162, 164, 194

1 John
3:1a	127

Revelation
19:16	146

Index of Topics and Categories

Passion/Palm Sunday 128-132. *Also:*

Holy Week 128-135. *Also:*

Easter 136-139. *Also:*

Ascension

Pentecost 140-143. *Also:*

All Saints Day

Thanksgiving Day

CHRISTMAS. *See* Christian Year

COMFORT

COMMITMENT

COMMUNION, HOLY 84-87. *Also:*

COMMUNITY IN CHRIST (FELLOWSHIP)

CREATION

DESCANTS

DISCIPLESHIP AND SERVICE 170-187. *Also:*

EASTER. *See* **Christian Year**

EPIPHANY. *See* **Christian Year**

ETERNAL LIFE (HEAVEN)

FAITH 162-169. *Also:*

FAMILY

FELLOWSHIP. *See* **Community in Christ (Fellowship)**

GRACE

GUIDANCE

HEALING

HOLY SPIRIT

140   God sends us the Spirit
74   Lord, listen to your children praying
75   O God in heaven
142   *Spirit, Come Down*

HOLY WEEK. *See* Christian Year

HOPE

86   Come to the table of love
92   May you run and not be weary

JESUS CHRIST

38   He came down
146   He is the King of kings
136   *He's Alive!*
21   *How Majestic Is Your Name*
174   I have decided to follow Jesus
10   *Jesu, Tawa Pano*
158   *Jesus in the Morning*
148   Jesus is a Rock
40   Jesus, Jesus, let us tell you
113   like a child
42   Lord, I lift your name on high
44   No other name but the name of Jesus
41   O for a thousand tongues to sing
75   O God in heaven
127   O how he loves you and me
46   Praise the Lord, all creation
114   Prepare the royal highway
178   *Rainbow of God's Love*
50   Shine, Jesus, shine
139   This is the day that the Lord has made
98   Two fishermen

JOY

172   Give me oil in my lamp
38   He came down
147   Ho-ho-ho-hosanna
175   I've got peace like a river
92   May you run and not be weary
52   Shout to the Lord
94   *The Trees of the Field*

JUSTICE

88   *Canto de Esperanza*
108   Dance and sing for the Lord will be with us
89   *Enviado Soy de Dios*

KINGDOM OF GOD

89   *Enviado Soy de Dios*
19   For the beauty of the earth
114   Prepare the royal highway
189   Walk with me

LENT. *See* Christian Year

LIGHT

22   God of mercy, God of grace
50   Shine, Jesus, shine
184   This little light of mine

LOVE

11   Come, let us gather
86   Come to the table of love
172   Give me oil in my lamp
38   He came down
175   I've got peace like a river
40   Jesus, Jesus, let us tell you
64   Love God with your heart
65   Praise the Lord, praise the Lord
178   *Rainbow of God's Love*
182   *The Sharing Song*

MERCY

22   God of mercy, God of grace

MISSION

88   *Canto de Esperanza*
89   *Enviado Soy de Dios*
22   God of mercy, God of grace
50   Shine, Jesus, shine
97   *Thuma Mina*
176   You are my Shepherd

MUSIC AND SINGING 159-161. *Also:*

60   *Cantai ao Senhor*
9   Come into God's presence singing
11   Come, let us gather
29   Make a joyful noise unto the Lord
30   Praise the Lord with the sound of trumpet
32   *Sing Alleluia*
34   Sing to the Lord

ORFF AND RHYTHM INSTRUMENTS

107   *Advent Candle Song*
11   Come, let us gather
90   Go now in peace
136   *He's Alive!*
10   *Jesu, Tawa Pano*
96   *Shalom*
32   *Sing Alleluia*
12   *Venid Cantemos*

PARTNER SONGS

144   *All Night, All Day / Chatter with the Angels*
188   *Da Pacem Domine*
20   *God Is So Good*
116   *Magnificat*
150   *Marchin' to the Beat of God*

PASSION/PALM SUNDAY. *See* Christian Year

PEACE, INNER

58   Be still and know that I am God
188   *Da Pacem Domine*
20   *God Is So Good*
175   I've got peace like a river
70   The Lord is my Shepherd

PEACE, WORLD

192   *A Brand New Day*
88   *Canto de Esperanza*
84   Circle the table, hands now extend

78 Take, O take me as I am
169 When I am afraid, I will trust in you

Sending Forth 88-97. *Also:*
190 Heveinu shalom alechem

SERVICE TO OTHERS. *See also* **Discipleship and Service**
182 *The Sharing Song*

SORROW AND GRIEF
20 *God Is So Good*

STEWARDSHIP
80 *Offertory Song*
126 The wise may bring their learning

STRENGTH AND COURAGE
16 Everywhere I go, the Lord is near me

TABLE BLESSINGS
18 For health and strength

TESTIMONY AND WITNESS 170-179. *Also:*
22 God of mercy, God of grace
41 O for a thousand tongues to sing
33 The heavens are telling the glory of God

THANKSGIVING
18 For health and strength
19 For the beauty of the earth
158 *Jesus in the Morning*
42 Lord, I lift your name on high
80 *Offertory Song*
32 *Sing Alleluia*

TRANSFIGURATION. *See* **Christian Year**

TRINITY
82 Come, be baptized
15 Father, I adore you
56 Glory be to God on high
75 O God in heaven
50 Shine, Jesus, shine

TRUST 162-169. *Also:*
58 Be still and know that I am God
20 *God Is So Good*

UNITY
192 *A Brand New Day*
84 Circle the table, hands now extend
86 Come to the table of love
19 For the beauty of the earth
59 *Hine Ma Tov*
137 Living Christ, bring us love
57 *¡Miren Qué Bueno!*

WORLD MUSIC

Argentina
57 *¡Miren Qué Bueno!*
88 *Canto de Esperanza*
77 *Santo, Santo, Santo*

Brazil
60 *Cantai ao Senhor*

Cameroon
38 He came down

Caribbean
36 Halle, Halle, Halleluja

China
85 *Jiu shi zhi shen*

Cuba
89 *Enviado Soy de Dios*

Gonja (Africa)
140 God sends us the Spirit

Hebrew Traditional
190 Heveinu shalom alechem
59 *Hine Ma Tov*
96 *Shalom*

Hispanic American
118 *Duérmete, Niño Lindo*
12 *Venid Cantemos*

Japanese
65 Praise the Lord, praise the Lord

Native American
49 Heleluyan, heleluyan

Phillipines
75 O God in heaven

South Africa
14 *Amen Siyakudumisa*
97 *Thuma Mina*

West Indies
124 The virgin Mary had a baby boy

Zimbabwe
10 *Jesu, Tawa Pano*

CD Track Index

CD Track Song List (In Order of Songbook)

CD 1 (pages 9-77)

PRAISING GOD

Gathering
1. Come into God's Presence Singing
2. Jesu, Tawa Pano
3. Come, Let Us Gather

Giving Thanks and Praise
4. Venid Cantemos
5. Amen Siakudumisa
6. Father, I Adore You
7. Everywhere I Go
8. For Health and Strength
9. For the Beauty of the Earth
10. God Is So Good
11. How Majestic Is Your Name
12. God of Mercy, God of Grace
13. He Has Made Me Glad
14. I Will Call upon the Lord
15. Joyful, Joyful We Adore Thee
16. Make a Joyful Noise unto the Lord
17. Praise the Lord with the Sound of Trumpet
18. Sing Alleluia
19. The Heavens Are Telling
20. Sing to the Lord
21. Halle, Halle, Halleluja
22. He Came Down
23. I Love You, Lord
24. Jesus, Jesus, Let Us Tell You
25. O For a Thousand Tongues to Sing
26. Lord, I Lift Your Name on High
27. No Other Name
28. Praise the Lord, All Creation
29. Rejoice in the Lord Always
30. Heleluyan
31. Shine, Jesus, Shine
32. Shout to the Lord
33. With My Whole Heart
34. Glory Be to God on High

God's Word
35. ¡Miren Qué Bueno!
36. Be Still and Know
37. Hine Ma Tov
38. Cantai ao Senhor
39. Come Bless the Lord
40. Love God with Your Heart
41. Praise the Lord
42. Luke 10:27
43. Seek Ye First
44. The Lord Is My Shepherd
45. Where Shall I Go from Your Spirit?

Prayer
46. Lord, Listen to Your Children Praying
47. O God in Heaven
48. Sanctuary
49. Santo, Santo, Santo

CD 2 (pages 78-135)

(Prayer, continued)
1. Take, O Take Me As I Am

Offering
2. Offertory Song

Baptism
3. Come, Be Baptized
4. Wonder of Wonders

Communion
5. Circle the Table
6. Jiu shi zhi shen
7. Come to the Table of Love

Sending Forth
8. Canto de Esperanza
9. Enviado Soy de Dios
10. Go Now in Peace
11. Lord, Make Me More Holy
12. May You Run and Not Be Weary
13. The Trees of the Field
14. Shalom
15. Thuma Mina

GOD'S STORY

Bible Stories
16. Two Fishermen
17. Silver and Gold Have I None
18. When Jesus Saw the Fishermen
19. Peter Rock
20. Jesus Called the Twelve Disciples

Advent
21. Advent Candle Song
22. Dance and Sing, for the Lord Will Be with Us
23. Holy Baby, Holy Child
24. Get Ready!
25. Light One Candle for Waiting
26. like a child
27. Prepare the Royal Highway
28. Magnificat

Christmas and Epiphany
29. Children, Go Where I Send You
30. Duérmete, Niño Lindo
31. Go, Tell It on the Mountain
32. Long, Long Ago
33. One Holy Night in Bethlehem
34. The Virgin Mary Had a Baby Boy
35. The Wise May Bring Their Learning

Lent
36. O How He Loves You and Me
37. Mantos y Palmas
38. Hosanna in the Highest
39. Dear Joseph of Arimathea
40. We Sang Our Glad Hosannas

CD 3 (pages 136-195)

Easter and Eastertide
1. He's Alive!
2. Living Christ, Bring Us Love
3. Mary Told the Good News
4. This Is the Day

Pentecost
5. God Sends Us the Spirit
6. Spirit, Come Down

GOD'S CHURCH

Celebration
7. All Night, All Day/Chatter with the Angels
8. He Is the King of Kings
9. Ho-Ho-Ho-Hosanna
10. Jesus Is a Rock
11. Marchin' to the Beat of God
12. Rock-a My Soul
13. The Body Song
14. Jesus in the Morning

Music and Singing
15. With My Voice
16. Now Is the Time

Faith and Trust
17. Faith
18. We Must Be Faithful
19. The Lord Is My God
20. When I Am Afraid

Witness and Service
21. Fruit of the Spirit
22. Give Me Oil in My Lamp
23. I Have Decided to Follow Jesus
24. I've Got Peace Like a River
25. You Are My Shepherd
26. Rainbow of God's Love
27. The Giving Song
28. The Sharing Song
29. This Little Light of Mine
30. The Peacemakers
31. Make Me a Servant

Community of God
32. Da Pacem Domine
33. Walk with Me
34. Heveinu Shalom Alechem
35. A Brand New Day
36. Saints Today, Saints of Old

Index of First Lines and Common Titles